Tasha Cavanag

Memories and Reflections of an Adoptive Mum

Story of a Multiple Adoption

A Memoir

Disclaimer

The stories in this memoir are true but reflect the author's recollection of events. Some names, locations and identifying characteristics have been changed to protect the privacy of those depicted. Dialogue has been recreated from memory.

Contents

Tasha Cavanagh

MEMORIES AND REFLECTIONS OF AN ADOPTIVE MUM.

Introduction

The writing of this memoir came out of a letter I wrote to my grown up adopted daughters when their biological mother came on the scene and who had told untruths about the adoption. Over the years I had protected my three abused and neglected daughters, all sisters from one family, from some aspects of their past, the adoption, threat of kidnap, and consequences of the abuse and neglect, which they all had experienced differently. This memoir shows how difficult it was to adopt and how my family traumas prior to the adoption prepared and motivated me to cope with a multiple adoption. In addition, why my expectations of a family life had to change post adoption, as we were dealing with very young children who come with a past.

There are always unexpected events that occur after adoption like coping with their biological parents, or meeting them for the first time. For me most of all I tried to protect my daughters from the difficulties I had experienced throughout their lives; a divorce, the difficulties of working with their father for two years after the divorce, his remarriage, and the consequences in helping my children grow to independence, and for them not to become one of the many adoptions that breakdown.

There were major emotional crisis's I had experienced throughout my life and with my daughters that I could not make sense of at the time, but became clear through understanding my family history and past experiences. Questions I have often been asked and ask of myself: What drove me to adopt three children all from one family and at the same time? Why did it feel so natural, when I had no siblings of my own? What has made me work so hard through all the enormous difficulties with abused and neglected children, when others would have given up years ago?

I could not explain to others or to myself the gut feelings that I had to keep the children together and stay connected to them throughout. I found some of the answers when I had to help my children with my family history, and found other answers whilst further investigating my family history in my retirement.

So how are my daughters now they have grown up with their experiences of partners, husbands, motherhood and their life? Their biological mother is now on the scene and both their fathers have died.

What has become of me now I have a life of my own, with a partner, study and travel, though I am never totally free from the problems from the girls? I can see that some of the problems today stem from their experiences prior to the adoption, post adoption and into adulthood. New research shows how these problems can stem from early childhood stress.

The subsequent part of the memoir is written in real time, from the consequences of Tiffany's Wedding Party in November 2019 when I met the biological mother.

I have three daughters, five grand-children and one great grandchild. Now, as a Great-Grandmother I feel compelled to write down these experiences and insights to help me understand myself. In addition, it is written to help today's professionals with the adoption process and its consequences. So too for those interested in dysfunctional families and family history. It is written for all prospective and current adoptive parents to help them cope and get support, but especially for adoptive mums of siblings in a multiple adoption.

Chapter 1

TO MY DAUGHTERS

From the letter to my daughters.

Why am I writing this for you now? I have become aware that your memories are limited by how young you were when we adopted you, by the appearance of your own biological mum, memories coloured by others over time, and questions you need the answers too but are too afraid to ask.

I fell in love with you all the moment when you first arrived at our house, standing in the lounge full of bewilderment, with each of you carrying a small cardboard box full of your worldly goods and dirty toys. Tiffany, a tiny dot, clinging to her dirty dogged eared panda. I looked at you and said I would need your help, as I had little experience with children. I continued to say you needed my help too, and I smiled, and you all nodded expectantly. We looked at each other not knowing of the enormous journey we would be undertaking together.

I was talking to Becca recently when I realised that their biological mum was telling her about the time of the adoption that wasn't true. Dave (my ex-husband) and his wife Scarlett had also told Becca things about me that were not true either. Stories that were confusing to all my daughters, so I decided to tell them how we became adoptive parents and about the adoption.

I did not realise, at the time, that my previous experiences and traumas helped me to prepare for, and motivated me to adopt, and to cope with subsequent traumas post adoption.

Chapter 2

BEGINNINGS AND TRAUMAS

My Background to Becoming an Adoptive parent

In 1972, I met Dave at the 18+ club on the Isle of Wight where I lived. I was 22, and my life up to then was helping to care for my very sick father.

My dad was ill on and off all my life, and often I came home from school to find he was in hospital. My mother could not cope with my dad's illnesses or operations, and did not like the frequent visits to whichever hospital my dad was in. I visited the hospitals after school and later became his main carer. My father became seriously ill in 1969, when I was 18 years old, and he had several abdominal operations one of which caused a pulmonary embolism, luckily he was in hospital or he would not have survived.

I changed from accounts and office work and went to work in a factory (as a ball and wick operator in Ronsons lighter factory), on the understanding that I could take time off to support my father in the 24 hours, each time he came home from hospital. Eventually, my mother and I took two jobs to help with the income. This went on for 3 years and I ended up with no breaks, or life of my own, as I was constantly working, visiting the hospital, caring for dad and supporting my mum.

Inevitably, I found it increasingly difficult to visit the hospitals and developed a phobia about vomiting and seeing people being sick. So, I went to the doctor and asked for help as I needed to keep going. The doctor suggested I saw a psychiatrist who treated these sort of problems, and I didn't care who I saw as I wanted to continue helping my father. The psychiatrist helped me to see that the real fear was expecting my dad not to be alive, each time I went to the hospital. The psychiatrist continued to be a great support to me and worked with one of my GPs who taught me hypnosis, to help me cope with the hospital visits where many people vomited after operations. I think deep down I was trying to keep my father alive which was a tremendous responsibility on me being so young.

Although my father eventually recovered he felt he was on borrowed time, and he decided it was time for me to have a life of my own, despite my mother's protestations. My life until then had revolved around work, visiting the hospital and caring for him when he came home. I was so busy, I had ceased to have friends. I was so shy by this time that my dad actually introduced me to the owner of a pub, where the 18+ group held events, and that is where I met Dave. Many years later I became aware that Dave and Scarlett, his new wife, told our daughters and others that I had an unhealthy relationship with my father, but I didn't. I was close to my dad as I had a major part in caring for him, as my mum couldn't cope with it all.

In 1972, I had a life with parties, making friends, and going to different events. Dave was a mobile disc jockey and lived in a flat on his own, he was attracted to me and I to him, and he wanted to go out with me. Dave was my first proper boyfriend, life seemed good, and at that point I did not realise I was about to enter a dysfunctional family.

Chapter 3

MARRIAGE AND FAMILY TRAUMA

Mother-in-law

Dave did not introduce me to his parents who were living on the Isle of Wight, for some months after we started going out together which seemed strange, but in my naivety I did not question it. I think I saw his parents a couple of times prior to Dave asking me to marry him and me saying yes in June 1974. A family feud ensued following our engagement, as his mum made it clear she did not like me. It appeared she did not like any of Dave's girlfriends, but focussed her hatred onto me as he was insistent on marrying me.

The problems became worse, I received poison pen letters, and my mum and dad kept receiving telephone calls from her saying that I was nothing more than her son had dragged off the streets. However, Dave was still insistent on marrying me, and I hoped his mum would get to like me. How wrong I was, and the poisoned pen letters continued! Looking back now I wondered why I stayed around, probably as I had had no previous boyfriends or their relatives to compare with.

Dave and I decided not to get married in a church as we both felt it to be hypocritical, it was then that his mum's hatred really began (as if what she had been doing wasn't enough). Dave's mum vowed to disrupt the wedding, she phoned Dave's work, and told his boss to sack him as he was marrying me. It appeared she hated me as I was not like his sister. I have a Report Form F, which is copy of our adoption application form which confirms this in Dave's own words, where he states 'after many traumas and hysterical scenes from my mother we finally got married in a registry office on the 30th of August 1974'. Dave and I decided to have a small wedding with just two witnesses agreed reluctantly by my mum and dad because of the disruption his mum could have caused.

As it was his mum did find out and she phoned the police on our wedding day telling them to stop the wedding. The police station was across the road from the registry office and a plain clothes policeman came across to tell Dave about his mother's phone call. The policeman told Dave not to worry as he had come over from the police station to give us the message that all the police in the station wished us every happiness, probably saying under his breath that we need it. That was in 1974, and as his sister and father stood by his mother Dave decided not to have contact with his family again. Dave was giving his mother up for me.

Family Deaths

In 1977, we were living and working in Wales where Dave was a lecturer in the plastics industry and I was working in an office for a construction company. One day in February I received a call that my dad was in hospital with a suspected cerebral bleed on the brain. Dave took me to the I.O.W and then returned to Wales. For the next two weeks I lived with my mum and every day I travelled to Southampton Hospital, where my dad had been transferred to the neurological unit, which my mum would not visit. I helped the nurses with other patients as they were short staffed, and sat with my dad talking to him about everything.

After two weeks he had a major main stem bleed whilst having a brain scan. I was on the I.O.W. when I received the call that he was dying and we had to try and get to Southampton Hospital quickly, and as usual my mum did not want to go, but I persuaded her. With the help of one of mum's work colleagues and the police asking for the hydrofoil to wait for us we got to Southampton, unfortunately too late. My father had died at the age of 50.

My father died in February 1977, then my paternal grandmother also died a few months later as did my father-in-law. These were the main deaths, there was another family member and old friend of mine who also died that year. It was at the end of the year that my husband discovered he could not have children. During this time I felt I was on another planet and on automatic pilot, as I had not enough time to grieve for one person before there was another death. I had helped arrange three funerals at the age of 26.

We made contact again with Dave's mother when his father died in the hope of reconciliation and to help her. However, I got the blame again from his mother for killing her husband because of the stress I had caused! Dave and I could not believe it, but we decided we would go to the funeral together. We were at Dave's mum's house the day before the funeral when the vicar arrived, he came up to me took my hands and said 'the black sheep of the family welcome back into the fold'.

It felt so surreal I started to cry, Dave's mum then came up to me and said 'that is what I have been waiting for now I can forgive you'. I did not understand 'Forgive me for what! I could not believe it I had already helped to arrange three funerals and I was devastated. Post script the vicar was drunk as a lord at the funeral!

No-one could believe what was happening, not even my psychiatrist who I had asked to see just once because I was beginning to feel responsible for what was happening, especially as my mother-in-law accused me of killing her husband. I just could not understand what was happening, but the psychiatrist reaffirmed that he had the wrong person sat in the chair. It was surreal as I had just lost the two most influential people in my life my father and my grandmother in quick succession. (See Chapter 15 Family History.)

It was later when Dave told me his mum previously had had psychiatric treatment at Maudsley hospital which finally explained a lot, and I had just wished he had told me earlier. Dave also told me that his mum so desperately wanted a girl, that he was dressed as a girl and called Sylvia, for the first two years of his life. Dave decided not to see his mother again after his dad's funeral, and gradually I came to terms with my losses with counselling help. However, Dave removed all the photographs of his and my family from view in our house. He wouldn't talk about his father, my father or his mother and suppressed it all, much to the detriment of our marriage long after we had adopted the girls.

The greatest disappointment to us both was not being able to have children and the tests showed that there was no possibility of Dave being able to father children. We discussed artificial insemination by donor but Dave said he could not bring up another man's baby that I had given birth too. Dave's doctor suggested adoption as an option which we discussed and explored, Dave liked this option because we would then both be equal as parents. My only condition was to wait about nine months to allow us come to terms with what we had been through, especially for me coming to terms with not being able to have my own baby.

Chapter 4

ADOPTION

Adoption Process

In 1979 we were living in a county near to Wales, with
Dave working as a manager in a plastics company, and we
decided to try for adoption. Subsequently, we contacted
several social services in different counties and Barnardo's
Adoption Agency, but it became obvious that we could not
adopt a small white baby, as there was a shortage and that
still applies today. It was also unlikely, we would be able to
adopt within the local social services because of the time it
takes to adopt in that county. We would have been too old
by the time the process would have been completed, as we
would have been in our thirties and we were both 28 at that
time.

However, we were invited by a Social Services in the
West Midlands to attend a series of discussion evenings
about adopting hard to place children and siblings. We went
to all the meetings, met other adoptive parents, and saw the
range of difficult to place children, including siblings up for
adoption, and my heart went out to them. Dave liked the

idea of a readymade family. In consequence, we started the long and comprehensive adoption process.

To become adoptive parents we had to have full medicals, chest x rays, police checks and background checks. We had to write lengthy reports on our life and attitudes to children, including children from different backgrounds, religions and cultures, and how we would cope with difficulties. We had several in depth interviews and everything was investigated. Neighbours were consulted and references checked.

I had to have a psychiatric evaluation and the psychiatrist fully supported my adoption application. My original psychiatrist gave me a glowing reference. Dave did not have to have a psychiatric evaluation! I did not question this at the time partly because I was told as the mother I would be the main carer of any children, or maybe it was because I had previously seen a psychiatrist and I just accepted it.

With hindsight it is a pity that Dave hadn't had to have an initial adoption interview with a psychiatrist, like I had too, who could have seen that he had not coped, or had come to terms with his family trauma and loss. This became apparent later when we went to marriage guidance and Dave explained to the counsellor and me that he had not wanted to continue with the adoption, as he could not cope with fostering the girls'. Dave did not say anything to the social workers at the time of the adoption, as he did not want to be perceived as a failure.

Perhaps getting a psychiatric evaluation should be mandatory for all adoptive parents because I now know that most older children, who get adopted, have some form of neglect or abuse in their background with problems that can appear later in life. This is further complicated in a multiple adoption with the communication and the dynamics of relationships between siblings.

I now know, from research from the Adoption and Fostering Agency, that babies adopted in short a time as 10 days can have difficulties, later in life, in forming appropriate close emotional bonds; it is called Rejection Theory (Adoption UK). Most children with these experiences will push their adoptive parents either one or both to reject them, as a continuation of their past.

Perhaps the clash with a child's past, the consequences of that past, and with the expectations of adoptive parents is why in the 1990s during my social work course 2/3 of adoptions broke down and now more than a 1/4 adoptions break down, with all the sadness and distress that brings to adoptive parents and the children.

I think social workers should be more honest that adoption is not just about giving children a stable home, or hope that love enough would conquer the trauma of their past experiences. The expectations for a family life are not explained and I think social workers should be more honest about an individual case of adoption. We had no follow up support as expected, though I believe some agencies do now provide after adoption support, I know others do not.

Becoming Adoptive Parents

But all that comes later in this story as at the time, in 1981, we were accepted as adoptive parents and were told by social services that they only placed hard to place children with people who have been through trauma, so we were ideal adoptive parents. Initially, there was a child with a minor disability coming up for adoption but the long term foster carers decided to adopt him themselves, as his brother and sister were in long term foster care within the same locality. Then a Chinese family of six came up for adoption, and whilst this was being explored our three girls came up as an emergency placement.

Today, children from different cultures, or mixed race children, try to be placed in whichever culture is within the child. Unfortunately, there is often a shortage of suitable parents and many children are either split up, put into long term foster care, or are languishing in care, without the love and support of a possible stable family (Muir & Moorhead 2010).

We were told by the social workers that the girls' had come to the attention of the social services as an emergency, and they had nowhere in long term care to place them, especially together, which the social workers thought was essential because of their experiences. So the social workers asked us if we would be willing to foster these girls, even though we were   adoptive parents and not foster carers. Under the circumstances we agreed. A newspaper report at the time from the Express and Star dated 12/8/81 explained the circumstances when they were first taken into care.

The headlines stated 'Unfed girls kept in dirty conditions'. The girls were seven, five and one and were living in shocking conditions. They were all unkempt and there was no food in the house except a few slices of mouldy bread. The house was dirty with the smell of urine and covered in dog faeces, and the youngest child had no nappy on. Nobody else was in the house and several complaints had been made by the neighbours that the children had been left all day and night. The children had not attended school and health visitors and social workers had not been allowed entry into the house.

The police eventually found the father in a pub and he stated that he 'was not prepared to give up his drinking and darts to look after the children'. The mother had left when youngest was four months old, then the father locked the baby in a bedroom in a cot, on a bare mattress that was soiled and smelt of urine, and there was only a dirty and empty feed bottle for her. In fact all the girls slept on bare mattresses which smelt of urine.

The social workers told us the mother had come back for a short period of time but left again without taking any of the children with her. The girls continued to be neglected, but the abuse they had suffered at the time did not become evident until after the adoption.

The police took the children into care in August 1981, but as they clung to each other like little frightened monkeys the social workers decided to keep them together, but could only find a very short-term foster placement for them. The temporary foster carers then wrote a report on all the girls.

Foster Carers Report

All the girls' had worms and Becca and Sian had to have extensive dental treatment. Tiffany, the youngest, was way behind in toilet training which wasn't surprising as she had 1 inch sores from nappy rash, and her clothes had to be burnt, as they smelt of urine even after several washes. Becca, aged 5, was a loner and was 12 months behind her class mates, she only knew six words, was slow getting dressed, and she stayed very close to Sian. Sian, aged 7, was very protective of her younger sisters, was very strong-willed, had moods and a temper. She too was 12 months behind compared to her class mates.

The temporary foster parents, within weeks, experienced difficulties between Sian and their own two children, who were of a similar age, as Sian wanted to be in control of everyone. It was then decided, by the social workers, that the girls should not be placed where there were other children in the family. So later in 1981 the social workers asked us if we would be willing to foster the girls with a view to adoption, and we said we would be pleased to help.

Initially we went to meet the girls several times at the temporary emergency foster carers where we were introduced to each other, and I talked to the girls' about school, bathed them, put them to bed, and read to them under the watchful eyes of the foster mum, who wrote an excellent report supporting us. Sian and Becca did chat to us but Becca was quiet in the presence of her sister. Tiffany did not say word, but kept doing amusing things like hiding her face in corner and turning around to make us laugh, but she never smiled or laughed.

Dave and I fully understood the girls may have had to return to their own mother, if the social workers could find her, and that both biological parents would have to be fully investigated before a decision could be made, as to what was the best future for the children. However, the social workers stipulated to us that we as adoptive parents would have no contact with their biological family, and that any contact needed would be with the girls alone under social services supervision. This was the legal position at the time.

The first year whilst fostering the girls was full of revelations, joy and emotional turmoil as we struggled to get to know one another. Health wise the girls' were all small in size and had evaluations from doctors and paediatricians who concluded that all of them were two years behind in their physical, psychological and educational development. Tiffany had the body weight of a nine month old baby, signs of rickets and scoliosis of the spine. Becca was small for her age because of malnutrition during a growth spurt and had hypoplasia on her teeth. Sian displayed behavioural problems, for example drawing pictures of jumping off mountains and being dead.

I wrote the following foster care report 10 months after having the girls' in my care.

At first Sian had difficulty forming close relationships with other children and, with Dave and me, and she wanted to take on the mother role to her two sisters, which was understandable. She did not trust grown-ups and needed to be a child again. Sian was undisciplined, unused to supervision, and had very severe temper tantrums if she could not get her own way. She was terrified of seeing her father again and it comes out later in her story as to why!

Becca was very clinging to start with and terrified that I would go out of her sight. She used to sulk for hours and more than anything she wanted a mother. Becca kept asking me 'Why did my mum leave me? And she needed constant hugs.

Tiffany used to scream and bite us to get our attention as she did not speak. She was frightened of her cot and in being put to bed. She was obviously scared to be left there for hours on end, as her biological father had done when he had locked her in the bedroom. Tiffany also screamed at her potty as Sian and Becca had tried to potty train her, bearing in mind they were only seven and five themselves. I left her using nappies for a while and eventually potty trained her, using our kitten we had for her to copy, then later she copied her sisters.

For bedtimes, sometimes I had to let Tiffany scream as my attention made it worse, but when she had calmed down I used to go in and snuggle her up in bed. Eventually, the screaming and crying stopped and she was happy to go bed. One day I bought Tiffany a little pair of red wellie boots and was totally surprised that after I told her to get ready for bed I found her clutching her little dog-eared panda, with her little red boots on the wrong feet. It was endearing as she was still not speaking.

There were fun times too as Sian and Becca eventually brought friends around to our house, and once we had thirteen children in our front garden. We went out regularly for runs in the park and the sunshine helped with their very pale complexions, especially for Tiffany. Sunshine with its vitamin D was good for Tiffany that helped her with her bone growth, and to conquer the development of rickets. We also went on regular trips outside to get all the girls into the fresh air. One trip, to Bewdley Wildlife Park, brought a smile to the faces of the girls', especially Tiffany because her ride in a train brought her first ever smile.

What the girls did not know was how much hard work the social workers, police, teachers, and health professionals, put into the court visits and the interim care orders continuing throughout this first year. With everyone committed to their future wellbeing and for them all to stay together. For the social workers this was to the first case of its kind, in this part of the country, for a multiple adoption of neglected and possibly abused children, as siblings had always been split up and placed with different foster parents.

We could not leave the children at all, not even with a babysitter, as during this time the social workers told us there was a threat of the girl's being snatched by the father, as he said he knew where his children were and the social workers had to believe him. I don't think my daughters, even now, are aware of how much the teachers, caretakers, parents at the school, and neighbours worked hard to protect them all when I was collecting them from different schools and activities.

Chapter 5

THE GIRLS BIOLOGICAL FAMILY

The Girls Background

It became apparent that the girls could not go home because their biological father had certainly neglected them, and, at the time the social workers could not trace their mother. So, in 1982, the social workers asked us to become the girls' adoptive parents and for us to start the adoption process. The social workers felt that all the girls' problems could be overcome with good nutrition and support. With hindsight, that was a very optimistic view, and Dave and I were rather naïve about the problems we would later encounter.

The law at that time stipulated that adoption severed all connections with the children's own family. Today, the law stipulates that some contact is to be maintained with the biological parents even if it's only a letter per year or a birthday card. To be honest I don't think I could have adopted under these circumstances, for whatever contact the children would have with their biological family, while they were young, would have undermined our attempts at a stable family life. We were adoptive parent's not foster carers. I think every case is individual, despite what the research shows, that overall some biological family contact helps children. I think that my case is a case in point.

The girls' were so young they may not remember what occurred during the long process to actually adopt them, but it was a nightmare.

The Biological Father and Threat of Kidnap

The girls' biological father was known to the social workers and the police as a fraudster, and a pathological liar with an aggressive personality. When he found out about the adoption process he attacked the social worker with a knife to his throat, and told him he would kill anyone connected with the adoption, and kill the kids rather than anyone else having them. The social worker was saved by use of the panic button, but no criminal action was taken at this point as far as I know. But the social worker did tell me, at one of his visits to us, that the police had to be present at all subsequent interviews.

The threat from the biological father to us all was taken seriously, and this was confirmed in a social work report, which I now have, that states the biological father's own father had previously reported his concerns to the social services department, and also states 'that his son would kill the kids'. Sian also became very distressed after seeing her biological father during one of the supervised sessions, because he threatened to kill her for letting the social workers into their house.

The threats were taken very seriously by the social workers, the police and the court. The girls' biological father decided to contest the case and three times he was invited to the court for a separate personal hearing and three times he failed to turn up. Meanwhile he said he knew where his girls' were, through knowledge given to him by a teacher at the girl's previous school because she felt sorry for him!

The biological father continually threatened to kidnap the girls' so we were all put on high alert, and we had to develop ways to protect them whilst at home and at school. I had to transport the girls' to school by car and take each of them into the school grounds where a teacher or the caretaker took them to class.

The other mums soon knew about this, and I could not believe it when they surrounded the girls' to protect them, if I was a little late collecting each of them from their schools. The neighbours too, kept me informed about any suspicious behaviour. The social workers had said their biological father had a blue van and we were to call the police immediately if we saw anything suspicious.

One day, my car broke down outside a house where a mum was holding her baby and I asked if I could use her phone (this was the days before mobile phones), and I said I know this is strange as explained why I could not walk the girls' to their schools. The mum said she knew all about us as family and she did not hesitate. She said "I will take you school so there is no need to phone" and with that she put her baby and us in her car and we did my normal school run. I could not thank her enough. The threat of the girls' being kidnapped was an enormous strain predominantly on me as Dave was at work.

Chapter 6

COMPLETION OF ADOPTION

Legal Process

We all had to have full medicals again for the adoption, and technically Dave and I were supposed to have a full medical, including chest x-rays, in relation to each child, but that was deemed excessive in our case. However, everything discovered had to be fully investigated, so I had to have a kidney, a bladder and bowel x-rays where my conditions were fully diagnosed. Luckily the results showed I had low bladder pressure and an overactive bowel, nothing that was serious enough to stop the adoption going ahead, but it was a very stressful time.

Meanwhile, the social workers, other professionals, and lawyers were working hard to provide the court with everything the court officials asked for. We were told that our case was a test case in the county for a multiple adoption of neglected children, who were being adopted, rather than firstly being split up and placed into long-term foster care. I have a copy of the test case where the social workers were trying to prove that the girls' adoption was essential to their long-term wellbeing.

The social workers were told by the court to make every effort to find their biological mother as the case was contested by their biological father. Dave and I knew very little of all the technicalities of the adoption. We did not know that the girls' mother eventually had been found, and had signed the adoption consent papers, until much later when the social workers told us. In addition, they told us that the man their mother was now living with had not wanted the girls' and that they now had a half – sister. Becca told me that their biological mum told her recently that we as adoptive parents were pushing for her to sign the papers, but we had nothing to do with it and it wouldn't have had anything to do with us.

The social workers gave us copies of all the reports and files with all the relevant information which came to us after the adoption, and this was unusual, but they thought it would help us with the girls' as they grew up, because of the complexity of this multiple adoption. In one of the reports it states that the girls' mother did return to them some months after she first left but then she left again two weeks later without them, but this report doesn't say why.

All it states is that the mother 'deserted' them all and the social workers could not initially find her.

We were given these social work reports including the history of their biological parents and court documents, in fact everything the social workers had on the case. This included the girls' individual reports, which each contains around a hundred pages of why they were taken into care, details of the numerous referrals, and subsequent reports. We gave Sian and Becca their reports when they were 18 but Tiffany did not want hers, I still have it, as she wants the put the past behind her, and the girls' may still not be aware of each other's detailed reports.

All of these reports were given to us prior to the Data Protection Act of 1988 which covers personal information that is used by organisations or government bodies. Today, these documents would not be given to adopted parents.

At the time of the adoption a Guardian ad Litum was appointed by the court to represent the children's interests, which meant he had the power to investigate everything, take up references, to talk to the girls' about our family life, and to do spot visits to check on us. On one such visit Becca and Sian eagerly told the Guardian ad Litum that I had fallen off a chair as I was drunk, giving the impression I was an alcoholic. I was mortified, but he laughed when I explained it was at Christmas, and I did have a drink but I had missed the chair. With all the medicals we were having he knew we weren't alcoholics. On another occasion he arrived whilst Tiffany was having a tea party with all her toys to which the Guardian ad Litum joined in, and Tiffany gave him a pretend cup of tea.

In addition, the headmistress of Becca's school and the headmaster of Sian's school had to submit reports to the court and the social workers, so they came to our house for a case review. Dave did not attend as he said he was working so I was at home with Tiffany. All I can remember from this case review was that Tiffany headed for the headmaster with a comb in her hand. I tried quickly to retrieve her but the headmaster gave his permission for her to sit on his lap. Eventually she stood up on him and combed very carefully his two strands of hair on his otherwise bald head. We all laughed as Tiffany was so funny.

Tiffany seemed to be attracted to father figures, which was understandable because of her experiences.

Adoption Hearing

In September 1982 a date was fixed for the adoption hearing, but special provision had to be made as their biological father was still threatening to kidnap the girls', and kill anyone related to their case. So, on the day we attended the court we had a police escort, the court was cleared of all people, and the police and clerk of the court monitored the situation. We were ushered into a room off the main courtroom where the judge was sitting, as he kindly thought being in a room would be less overwhelming for the girls', and less onerous on us. In attendance was the Guardian ad Litum and the clerk of the court.

We all sat quietly whilst the judge read some notes then Tiffany asked; 'Why has he got a cat on the table mummy?' She was referring to the Judge's wig, to which we all including the Guardian ad Litum and the clerk of the court started to laugh. When the judge looked up and realised what happen he stroked his wig and said to Tiffany 'it does look like a cat'. Sian then said 'it is a good job he is not wearing it on his head'. That broke the ice and the legalities of the case were read, the judge approved the adoption and wished us every happiness in the future.

We left the court again with a police escort to check we were not being followed, and by this time our now three daughters were giggling and thought it all was a good game. The judge approved the court order for the adoption and on September 2nd 1982 we became the girls' legal parents.

It appeared that their biological mother was eventually found via the benefit system, in a different geographical area, and she had signed the papers giving her consent on the 2nd of March 1982, which we knew nothing about until the adoption hearing. The judge agreed the adoption on the ground that their biological father was unreasonably withholding his consent and the biological mother had signed the consent papers, and that we were the right adoptive parents for these girls. The decision was made by the social workers and the court for the welfare of the children which was paramount.

Chapter 7

POST ADOPTION

Family Times and Past Experiences

The threats to us from their biological father continued for a while after the adoption so we never left them with a baby sitter. Life began following a usual pattern of school for Becca and Sian, and mother and toddler group and eventually playgroup for me and Tiffany. Tiffany being so small was continuously being dressed up in dolls clothes by the other children. However, the more settled the girls' became the more behavioural problems appeared, stemming from their experiences prior to Dave and I having them. In their own way they were telling me about what happened to them when they were at home with their biological father, some of which I was aware of as I now had their notes and reports of how they were taken into care.

At mealtimes I was trying to get my daughters to eat vegetables which they did, when they were plastered in tomato ketchup. The girls' chatted away and explained how there had been no food in their other house, except mouldy bread, and Sian explained she had to steal money from her biological father to buy her sisters some chips when their father was out of the house. I know this to be true because of the case and newspaper reports.

Some of the stories, however were harrowing, for example, Becca said and confirmed by Sian that she was hit by her father when she was trying to put a nappy on Tiffany, and she accidently stuck the pin in her. Becca was just five at the time and was trying to help her sister. I don't believe their biological father's hit was just a smack either knowing of his violent personality.

Some stories at the time may not have been true, so I got them to draw whatever they wanted and I put the pictures around the walls in the lounge as a talking point. This was one way I could help the girls' to come to terms with their past experiences. There were also fun times too when they drew around each other and their new friends.

I will not go into full details of their condition going into care as it is too much to add here, and their reports are personal to each of them. I know what they are so I suggested to the girls' that they read each other's reports to get an understanding of how it was for each of them, and for us as new parents, but I still do not know if they have done that.

Meanwhile I worked very closely with the teachers at Becca's and Sian schools. Becca was 5 years old and was initially scared of her teacher Mrs Trumper, a rather large lady. I just told Becca that her teacher was just a big teddy bear. The headmistress laughed and said I have never heard her been called that before and the teacher laughed too. Between us we got Becca settled in school where she started to learn. Both Becca and Sian wrote all their letters and words backwards. The teachers gave extra support to the girls with support of the headmistress at Becca's school and the headmaster at Sian's school, and I liaised with them all and between us the girls improved. I also continued getting them to read and write at home.

The girls' began to catch up at school and thrive, and they each had their own friends which was good. They also had their own interests over the years; Tiffany enjoyed ballet, but got expelled at the age of three because she influenced others into playing around. The teacher said to me 'I don't think your daughter is suitable for ballet' I didn't know whether to laugh or tell off Tiffany. However, she loved gymnastics and eventually football. Becca liked Brownies, playing the guitar and did part of the Duke of Edinburgh Award Scheme and Sian liked Art and Drawing, BMX and Football. In holiday time I took them to different places and local sites, and as a whole family we had holidays, from the Isle of Wight to Scotland. But a crisis time was looming!

Chapter 8

REDUNDANCY

Crisis Time

It was however, a difficult life for us all as just after the adoption in 1982, Dave was made redundant and Sian's behaviour was becoming a problem with attention seeking. We did not have any back up or support, as our social workers had moved on, or were retired, and the agencies did not want to know. The social services, where the girls' were adopted, said they were now out of their geographic jurisdiction, and the local social services said the girls' were the responsibility of the social services of the original adoption. In consequence, we never had any follow support. I understand now support is standard practice with some adoption agencies, but not with all.

I also understand from recent research that Government funding is available for adoption support, but this money is given to each local authority and distributed by them. I do not think this information is widely known and certainly not by some adoptive parents in need (Adoption UK 2020).

There was no funding or support for us at the time of the adoption or in post adoption.

Dave, also was not honest in that he did not want to adopt the girls' after he fostered them. This explained why he had left me looking after them, especially at the time of his redundancy, early after the adoption, and at a time when we also had to start up and run a business together. Soon after Dave was made redundant there was a prospect of us having to move. We certainly did not want to do that as our daughters were just settled into schools. I asked Dave what he really wanted to do and he said he wanted to set up his own business, so I said we would do just that.

After my dad died my mother gave me a stamp collection (all legally gifted) that was not sold at the time of his death, so I got it valued and I sold it for £15,000 and I put the money in to start up the business. Half of the money was matched by the bank and the remainder to support us for six months. If after six months the business failed to succeed we would have had to move, but it succeeded.

It was hard going as we set the business up from scratch with both of us as company directors. We started with two old second hand plastic injection moulding machines which we both, stripped down, cleaned, got working, and we were very busy working night and day. These machines were huge, I got inside one to clean out the sump oil, and both machines needed a lot of work. I named these machines Hinge and Bracket.

Eventually at the end of 1982, we became a limited liability company but with a second mortgage on the house. I always worked in the company from 9 to 3, then I would pick up the girls' from their schools; I would give each of them time to tell me anything and I would look at and check their homework. I would cook dinner and then often Dave and I would work in the evenings after the children were in bed, sometimes until one in the morning.

There was 24 hours responsibility when running this business, possibly that applies to any business, but I was beginning to have 24 hours responsibility for childcare as well. I was also unaware of a developing issue with money, when Dave insisted I was only to have the equivalent of a third of his wages out of the company, which I did not question at the time.

Chapter 9

THE GIRLS' BEHAVIOUR/POST ADOPTION

Funny Times

Meanwhile the girls' were improving at school and health wise, and we had some funny times with them when they all were playing on the fact that they were adopted. Sweets were put through our letter box because they told their friends that they had been starved. Other times they went to friend's houses and when they came home for dinner I found that they already had a meal, in fact Sian had already had two meals in one day. Becca also had a recorder given to her by a friend without parental consent because she had told her friend we lived in poverty. I obviously had to stop this as some of the mum's thought I given the girls my parental consent, but I did not know anything about what the girls' were doing. It was then that all of us mums' realised we were being played.

We had to take Tiffany when she was about three to an Injection Moulding Machine Fair in Birmingham, but for Health and Safety reasons the staff would not let us take her around with us, but the office staff offered to look after her. When we returned Tiffany was tucking into a box of Quality Street. The staff explained that their boss had come around in anger to tell off the staff about something. He sat down next to Tiffany and whilst he was in mid-flow Tiffany looked up and said him 'Do you like my drawing?' To which he turned around to her and said 'yes' and he gave her his business card.

The staff were delighted with Tiffany as she had diffused the whole atmosphere. Apparently the boss left in a better mood and Tiffany was fussed over. When we returned it appeared she had eaten two rounds of ham sandwiches and half a box of Quality Street. Though she was small Tiffany did have a big appetite. Later when Tiffany went to school I could understand why the dinner ladies kept giving her second helpings.

Behavioural Problems

Later all the girls' displayed behavioural problems. I was called to the school to pick up Becca where she had become hysterical during a thunder storm, and had set off mass hysteria in the whole class. I picked her up and she clung to me so tightly I had bruises. Later I discovered that their original house had been burgled whilst they were in bed, and they had huddled together as they were scared of the noise. Hence, Becca's anxiety about thunderstorms and her fear of the dark. But, the burglary was not true as it appeared their biological father, who told them about the burglary, had taken and sold a lot of their toys for money, probably to go drinking.

Becca was also anxious and clinging and often cried into my shoulder asking; 'Why did my mummy leave me?' I hugged her and I said 'I don't know darling but I would never leave you', as I tried to reassure her. I did not know that Becca would not remember any of these times throughout her childhood, and this would create problems, for me, later in life when the biological mother came on the scene, as Becca believes her over me. (See Chapter 19).

Tiffany and Sian were now having severe temper tantrums. I got so bruised from them my doctor thought I was a battered wife! Sian was also lying, stealing, cheating, being disruptive, argumentative, and bossing Tiffany. We were aware of more severe problems with Sian as she screamed when first attending church with the school, as she would not walk over the grating at the entrance, and the teachers had difficulty pacifying her. At home she ran out of the room when certain pictures came on the television. Sian later disclosed that she and her sisters were up most of the night, without their biological father in the house, watching horror movies and programmes showing adult scenes, and she also had seen pornographic magazines under her biological father's bed.

There was a possibility that Sian might have been sexually abused by the behaviour she was displaying, including suicidal thoughts. Perhaps the abuse was not by her biological father, as the social workers had previously told me that a teenage boy babysitting the girls' had spent time in Borstal, and one of the reasons was for sexually assaulting a 13 year old girl, and he was with all my daughters. This possibility was later confirmed, as written in the case notes where it was reported that a teenage boy was found babysitting all the girls', and at the time the social workers did not feel this was appropriate.

The Borstal System was abolished, under the Criminal Justice Act, in 1982 and replaced with Youth Custody Centres (Warwick University 2020). We do not know how this boy came to be babysitting all the girls'.

Dave could not accept the possibility of Sian being sexually abused, or cope with her behaviour, and retreated to work. Sian's behaviour was becoming difficult to handle, and she kept sitting on the upstairs window threatening to jump when she could not get her own way. Luckily my GP understood my concerns and gave me support, so too the teachers at Sian's school, however her behaviour continued to be difficult and became more acute as time went on.

Chapter 10

MARRIAGE DIFFICULTIES

Dave's Behaviour

Dave, meanwhile was becoming physically distanced from the girls' and emotionally distanced from me saying he was busy at work. However, that wasn't the case as later, when we had marriage guidance, he said he found he couldn't cope with the girls' whilst we were fostering them, and he didn't want to go through with the adoption, but couldn't admit it. The situation was deteriorating at home. Dave became jealous and controlling of me, he denied me access to our joint account and became demanding, at a time when the girls' were all having behavioural problems from their past experiences. This was not what I expected family life to be like.

For example, at home one day Sian and Tiffany were having temper tantrums at the same time. I had Tiffany under one arm to avoid her kicking me whilst trying to detach Sian from the radiator she was trying to pull off the wall, and Becca was clinging to my leg in her anxiety at her sisters being out of control. I had just got the girls' settled and was having a well-earned cup of tea when Dave arrived home and was angry because his dinner was not on the table, and continued to complain even after we sat down for the meal. It was then that I threw my dinner up to the ceiling which left a gravy stain, which the girls' all delighted in pointing out to their friends when they visited. It was then I decided that Dave and I needed marriage guidance, and this was in 1984.

It became apparent that Dave was also suffering from some of the effects from the separation from his own family, so in desperation I contacted his mother to try and save our marriage. I did get blamed again for killing her husband and I was now accused of keeping our three daughters away from her. However, we came to an arrangement where Dave would contact his mother and take the girls' to visit her, but without me.

I cannot remember why I consented or allowed his mother to treat me this way. All I remember is having strong sense of duty and an overwhelming commitment to try to keep the family together, especially as we had adopted the girls' and we had chosen them 'warts and all'. Dave visited his mother with the children many times, and I remember each time a twinge of jealousy, but I never said anything to the girls.

Unfortunately Dave overtime became more like his mother and I became more like my father and our relationship deteriorated. Dave became more jealous and controlling of me, I had to ask him for money as we had a joint account, and I had to account for every penny I spent, even for buying underwear. I was under such emotional strain that I got to the point of contacting the Citizens Advice Bureau (CAB) for advice, and was told that Dave's behaviour was almost like mental cruelty.

I decided to ask all my friends and relatives for money, as opposed to gifts for my birthdays and Christmases, and I opened an account in my own name, and when Dave found out he was livid. I think today Dave's behaviour would be classed as emotional abuse I however, eventually in 1986, on my birthday, I got a divorce on the grounds of Dave's unreasonable behaviour. I just felt relief.

By this time, though, I was beginning to blame myself for everything, which obviously in reality could not be true. It was the marriage guidance counsellor who made me realise that the breakdown of my marriage could not be all my fault. So, I really thought about the future, for me to cope with my daughters, without any of them having to go back in care. Now I that I felt stronger, I devised some strategies and demanded what I wanted to happen.

Divorce and Post-Divorce

Dave implied he would distance himself from the girls' after the divorce, but part of the divorce proceedings was the custody of children, and Dave wanted me to have sole custody. I however, made it plain to him, through a solicitor, that as much as I wanted to keep all the girls' I wouldn't be able to cope, and there was a risk of one or all of the girls' going back into care. That was a failure Dave could not admit too, so with the help of the judge and the court we were granted a co-parenting arrangement. We agreed I would continue working in the company, and Dave would pay the child maintenance to support our daughters.

I was able to cope with this arrangement as I had joined Gingerbread for lone parents, and I now had support and could start to build a life of my own, but with my daughters. The working arrangement continued until Scarlett came on the scene two years later, when Dave wanted me out of the company and Scarlett in!

This was a time when everything got really messy and I tried very hard to protect the girls' from what was happening. Meanwhile Sian's behaviour was deteriorating, she was truanting and bullying people at school, and was trying to bully her sisters at home. The actual timing of events is confusing me, so I will start with what happen in the business.

The Business

I was now only part-time in the business, to do the accounts and pay the wages. I was looking after the girls' and studying, which I had always wanted to do, from a suggestion by the marriage guidance counsellor, to create some distance and independence. My salary, however, was paid in the form of a cheque which Dave had to sign and he did, but by the time I went into the bank to pay the cheque in Dave had stopped it. Arguments ensued, but Dave continued to be difficult. It got to the point where I had to get help from the bank manager, where he suggested I paid the cheque into the bank two or three minutes prior to the bank closing, and he informed his staff to give me the help I needed. It was then too late for Dave to stop the cheque, even though he continued trying.

I had also noted some irregularities happening within the company, and it seemed that Dave was supplying Scarlett with our customer's details to help her with sales for an

Insurance Company, of whom she was working for. To me that was unethical and suggested some sort of insider trading. I was livid. I went into the company one day whilst Dave and Scarlett were there, and exercised my rights as a Company Director to investigate the whole of the business and noted irregularities. Dave and Scarlett did not like it, and Dave contacted the company solicitor, but he was told legally he could not stop me.

I desperately tried to keep these problems away from my daughters, but it was a very stressful time for me, and Sian's behaviour continued to deteriorate. I had to get help, as financially it was difficult for me to manage, so with a solicitor's advice I planned in 1988, to exit the company with my full rights and entitlements.

Meanwhile Sian started bullying her sisters especially Tiffany, so they had to be split up, and Dave took Sian to live with him, so we could protect the younger two sisters. That is when Dave really started being nasty to me, he threatened me by saying that I would never see Sian again unless I signed the company over to him. If I didn't then he would close the business down, and walk away from us all. Dave said to me that he had told his solicitors that I was over reactive and mentally ill, as I had seen a psychiatrist in my past!

An appointment had been made for us to discuss the company and my exit with solicitors, tax consultants, and a legal representative to represent the company. Dave was thinking I was going to sign the company over to him without any cost to him, or the company, but he had underestimated me. I had taped his threats to me about the company and in me not seeing Sian again, and I placed the tape on the table between us. I offered to play it, but I knew no one could listen to it as it could be deemed entrapment, but I said it was there to prove the blackmail existed and to show I was not mental!

Dave went white and the solicitors asked if I wanted to continue with the meeting, and I said yes. I laid down my conditions: I wanted the company to continue to keep the staff employed, I wanted a clean break with my share, as a sum paid to me on the current market value of the company, and I wanted the second mortgage lifted from my house. I wanted child maintenance to be paid directly out of the company, so Dave would continue to support our daughters.

Whilst Dave and his solicitors were thinking about this my solicitor made it clear to me that if the arrangements didn't work out I could get advice from a barrister, and he suggested I was quite capable of going to the Lincoln Inn Fields in London to see a barrister. His comments gave me a great confidence boost. However, visiting London was not necessary because after much discussion between Dave and his solicitor I got everything I asked for. So on the 8th December 1988, I left the company for good.

I worked so hard to keep our daughters together and for the co-parenting arrangement to continue. I never ran down their father or Scarlett, who was now trying to be a perfect stepmother to the girls'. I was committed to my daughters, I still loved them and in my mind always put them first, even as adults, much to my own detriment, but that comes later in my story. At the time Sian's behaviour was deteriorating. In the years that followed my leaving the company I would often have police at my door in the middle of the night and social workers on the phone, as Sian played truant from school and ran away from Dave and Scarlett. Eventually Dave put Sian into the local children's home and he would not have anything to do with her.

Chapter 11

SIAN'S BEHAVIOUR

Sian in Care

I can't remember the exact timing of events whilst Sian was in the Children's home, but they included Sian helping to steal a car and joyriding, which involved her in an accident where she ended up in hospital. I was contacted by the police and told that the driver had run off leaving Sian trapped in the car, which she had to be cut out of by the fire brigade. In addition, I was told that she was paralysed from the neck down. This was at night and I could not leave the house because of the two younger girls being in bed. I phoned Dave, and he did go to see Sian but found out that she was only bruised, which was a relief (See Chapter 18).

Sian also made many suicide attempts, most of which was attention seeking. However these attempts put a strain on us all, and I was going to the hospital on a regular basis. One day I took Tiffany to show her Sian attached to machines in the hope that she would not follow Sian's behaviour. There is a complex and powerful relationship between Sian and Tiffany, as Sian used to make Tiffany feel guilty and manipulate her by saying she was the one that saved Tiffany when she was little. Logically this was not true as

Sian was aged only seven when the girls' were taken into care, but up to then she did have some responsibility towards her sister. Sian hasn't had to care for Tiffany since 1981, but can still generate guilt in her.

The suicide attempts did ease after Sian asked me to go to the hospital to support her, not for her suicide attempt, but for her friend, who was in hospital seriously ill after she took Sian's pills at Sian's house. I pointed out to Sian that her feelings of distress about her friend were that same as those feelings we had in the family, after her own suicide attempts. Tiffany has never attempted suicide and neither has Becca, as far as I know.

Sian often ran away from the care home, and as usual I would be called on by the police day or night. There were bomb hoaxes, bullying of others, Sian broke someone's nose, lied, stole and cheated. Most serious were the arson attacks, the worst time was when there was a fire in her room at the children's home, and everyone including the fire brigade suspected Sian was the arsonist, as the fire was deliberate (See Chapter 18).

Dave had abandoned Sian at this time, so I visited her in the children's home, but I wasn't totally convinced that she had started the fire, as she had lost the picture of her biological mum, which she had kept close to her. Sian had however, certainly upset others at the home with her bullying, and the staff had real difficulty controlling her. As the fire could have caused a member of staff to be seriously injured or worse there was talk of Sian being placed into a secured unit, but Sian was terrified of this happening. Eventually there was not enough evidence against her to send her to a secured unit. Sian meanwhile was introducing me to her boyfriends, some of whom had just come out of prison for armed robbery.

However Sian was later involved with others in an arson attack at a school. Those involved including Sian were caught by the police, but it could not be determined who had actually started the fire. However, Sian subsequently was not charged, as it was established by the police that she was only an onlooker. Arson or a fascination with fire is known by experts as a behavioural response to childhood sexual abuse. But she has never openly disclosed any sexual abuse to us (See Chapter 18).

I tried to get help for Sian from a specialist psychologist, but she would have none of it. Dave did not want anything to do with Sian at this time, and Sian was trying to influence Becca's behaviour whilst threatening to kidnap

Tiffany from school. I could not cope with following Sian's behaviour, protecting her sisters' and their behaviour on my own. So, after a family discussion, with the help of Family Conciliation, it seemed appropriate to keep the younger two sisters apart to protect them. Dave subsequently agreed to have Becca and she went to live with him and Scarlett, whilst I continued to look after and protect Tiffany. The co-parenting arrangement continued even though it was complicated. There seemed to be a pattern emerging between Sian's behaviour, at this time, with that of her biological father's original threat of kidnap, but I don't think she or I recognised it then.

Perhaps the Jesuits were right when they said 'give me a boy until he is seven then I will give you the man'. I think this also applies to girls from my experience as Sian was seven when we adopted her. These patterns of behaviour could also explain why so many adoption breakdowns happen to other older adopted children too (See Chapter 18).

Sian in After Care

Sian was now, because of her age, having to leave the care home and was housed in her own flat near to Becca, and there was contact between them unbeknownst to us parents.

Sian was now trying to get Becca to leave school, not take any exams, and to go and live with her, which Becca eventually did. There was nothing Dave or I could do, as the relationship between both girls was far stronger than any bond with us.

Around this time the social workers always called on me to help with Sian, and whilst I was around they expected me to be involved, and because of it I could not get any other help. I was being called night and day about a problem with Sian, and co-parenting was still difficult with Dave and Scarlett, as they were now blaming me for Sian's behaviour.

Looking back, with hindsight, it is obvious that I alone could not be held for Sian's behaviour. However I was feeling some responsibility just like I did when Dave's mother had accused me of killing her husband. It was not logical, but at the time my feelings were overwhelming me because I was getting stress from all directions, from Sian, from Dave and Scarlett, from the social workers, and from the other girls' behaviour too.

Chapter 12

IMPACT OF SIAN'S BEHAVIOUR ON ME

Major Changes

However, all the girls were suffering and their behaviour was coloured by their past experiences, so I contacted the Adoption and Foster Agency, and got research papers on rejection theory and behavioural problems, whilst I was trying to get specialist help for Sian (See Chapter 18). I, however, was suffering from exhaustion, especially from Sian's behaviour, to the point I knew I had to physically get away.

I could see that I did not have a 'normal' family life with Becca or with Tiffany, and hadn't for such a long while; with my preoccupations with the business, Dave and Scarlett's attitude towards me, and with Sian's behaviour. I did try and help Becca and Tiffany as much as possible, with school and to get to know their life and their friends, but later it was an uphill struggle. The younger sisters were both very close and responded more to Sian than to me, probably because of their past and Sian had a way of generating guilt in them. (See Chapter 18).

Today, I can see how Tiffany must felt alone at times as my emotional time was taken away from her, because of the stress of the business, Sian's behaviour, and in her being so much younger than her sisters. I can also see how this contributed to her need to be independent. (See Chapter 18). However, Tiffany was the baby I never had, I loved her dearly and I still love her. Tiffany's feelings of rejection must have been compounded, when I finally moved away from the county, though I did give her a choice to live with me. I just couldn't cope anymore with Sian's Behaviour, and Dave and Scarlett's blaming me for everything that had happened.

I had two best friends, Lyn and Annette whom I had met on a counselling course as part of my studies. But when Lyn, now a social worker for the local Social Services, said her boss wanted her to become Sian's family social worker, she agreed. Annette, now a youth counsellor, said she wanted to become Sian's counsellor. I think they were trying to be helpful, but instead of feeling helped I suddenly felt betrayed by both of them. For a start you never get professionally involved in cases with family or friends; it is regarded as a conflict of interests. In addition, how could I have had conversations with my friends or feel supported by them, as I would have felt I was being continually judged by them. I felt I had lost my only support.

This was in 1992, after four years of struggling with difficult co-parenting after leaving the company. I struggled with conflicting obligations between, family, duty and my needs. I was feeling so overwhelmed by being constantly in demand, especially by the social workers wanting my help with Sian. I realised I could only get professional help for Sian if I left the County. I too now needed to get physically away for my own wellbeing and to support all my children. Though the idea filled me with guilt and excitement.

I originally looked for professional counselling courses, as I was now a trained counsellor and wanted to develop a career, but the courses I needed cost £10,000 which I could not afford. I would also need to be away for months on hospital or community placements, and that made me feel guilty. I thought that by studying social work at a university, I would be of more help to my daughters, I would be entitled to a student loan, and I could have an eventual career of my own; it was not a good idea however logical, but that comes later.

Dave and Scarlett created uproar when I suggested I was moving away to Oxford, so I contacted the Family

Conciliation Service again and we had meetings to discuss it. They said co-parenting long distance was a good idea for my sake, and I was going to show Tiffany other opportunities that could give her more independence, away from the influence of Sian.

I discussed this fully with Tiffany before I applied to university and I said I would stay around, until she was about 16, but she said no as she would feel very guilty about delaying my move. I think Tiffany could see I was struggling with everything. So I gave Tiffany the choice and opportunity to come and live with me, or stay with her dad and around her sisters, and she decided she wanted to stay. We finally arranged a long distance co-parenting agreement with Family Conciliation, approved by the court, and I went to Oxford in 1993 to study social work.

I could not discuss, in detail, my reasons for leaving the county with Becca or Sian because of their influence on Tiffany. Becca then about 18, and Sian about 20, did not ask me any questions as to why I was leaving, probably as they both had left home, and because of the complications in their relationships with us as parents. Later I found out they thought I was abandoning them like their biological mother! (See Chapter 18).

My choice of Oxford to study was because my daughters had loved Oxford when we visited, and I thought they would know where I was whilst I was away from them. After a parents evening with Dave, Tiffany told me of her delight at telling her teacher that I was studying at university in Oxford, when the teacher asked her where I was. Becca at 18, took on a mother's role and told me to behave myself at Uni. I replied that students usually take their washing home to their mother and I asked her if she would like my dirty washing, and she spluttered. So, it comes as a complete surprise to me as to what happens later on in the story under Becca's letter (See Chapter 20).

I was not aware at the time, of the consequences of protecting the girl's from everything that had gone on between Dave and me, or in my relationship with each of them. There was no guide book to help me. I was not aware of the complications and complexity of multiple adoptions, nor of the normal behaviour of brother and sisters in creating stories amongst themselves; as I had been an only child. In consequence of having no knowledge or previous experience I was struggling to constantly to do what I thought was the right thing as a parent. I did not know that Becca and especially Sian had influenced Tiffany into feeling I had totally abandoned them. I just thought I was making the right decision for all of us, but my decision backfired on me much later, particularly when their biological mother came on the scene.

Chapter 13

CONSEQUENCES AFTER MY MOVE TO OXFORD

Move to Oxford

It all didn't quite work out as planned after Family Conciliation and I had moved. Dave was becoming more like his mother, he was a now church goer, a bell ringer, and became a parent governor of Tiffany's school. When I had left the county Dave, Scarlett and Sian kept telling Tiffany what a bad mother I was and how I left her like her biological mother did. However, Tiffany was older, not the 4 months old when her biological mother had deserted them, and Tiffany was involved in the discussions of the move and had choices. In addition, her sisters had grown up and had left home. However, I can also see how my move must have influenced Tiffany and compounded her feelings of rejection.

I have since discovered that babies rejected at birth, or soon after can feel rejection, much more acutely than others when they reach their teenage years. This information is in the papers on Attachment Theory (See Chapter 18). I do not know if Tiffany remembers but we did have some good times in Oxford together. I took her to Windsor, London and Oxford, to shops, museums and the countryside. We drove past Eton College just as all the boys in their gowns came out of the college, and Tiffany's eyes came out on stalks!

I had many calls from the social workers during my social work training and I was asked to attend a case review on Sian, as I think Sian was pregnant at the time in 1994. I started to feel guilty again as I did not want to go to this case review. I talked to my tutor about my conflict and he said don't go, which I thought was a bit unusual from a social work trainer. Sian never attended the case review either. Sian had Caitlin when I was 43 and I became a grandmother.

Tiffany eventually followed the same pattern as Becca, and she too left school without taking exams and started living with Sian. I never knew why all the girls left Dave and Scarlett, or the reasons the younger sisters went into care prior to living with Sian. Becca then left Sian to live with her boyfriend. However, when Tiffany was living with Sian, Caitlin started calling Tiffany mummy instead of Sian. Tiffany, Becca and others became concerned and started phoning me about Sian's behaviour with Caitlin.

The worse time was when they told me that Sian had been dangling Caitlin over the balcony, one-handed by her baby grow, whilst Sian was under the influence of drugs.

Several of Sian's friends wanted to tell me about Sian's behaviour, so I could do something as they did not want to 'grass' on her directly to the social services. I contacted the NSPCC who told me to contact the social workers directly, and tell the social workers that Tiffany had been looking after Caitlin and that Becca was also looking after Caitlin at times. Anyone who reports suspected child abuse to the social services, however, gets investigated themselves in case they are being malicious. My social work training was useful as I could now talk to social workers on an equal level, but I was still fully investigated as to my reasons for letting the social worker know what was going on in Sian's flat.

The resultant case review went on without Sian or myself in attendance, but I did get a copy post the case review: It stated that the social worker had received numerous referrals about Caitlin and not just from me. But they concluded that Caitlin was well looked after by Sian, though Sian might need a bit of respite care because of financial difficulties.

The social workers had visited Sian when Tiffany wasn't there, and stated that Sian was a good mother as Caitlin was well looked after, and they didn't believe me about the situation with the drugs. The social workers only looked at the situation from Sian's point of view and would not look at the dynamics of the three sisters together. I was furious because the social workers would not listen to me for the protection of my granddaughter: I had no help or support from the social workers just like after the adoption.

Later Becca started looking after Caitlin as Sian went into a psychiatric hospital for a while. Sian was supposed to give Becca money for Caitlin, but did not, and Becca was getting desperate, so she asked for my help. I tried to get help from the local social services to get the financial support that Becca needed, but Caitlin was immediately taken from Becca and placed into foster care. The social services could not give Becca any money as she was not officially looking after Caitlin, though the social workers always wanted extended family to help. Becca became so distraught and I was fuming because we had only asked for help and support.

It appears from research that other families, even today, experience a lack of support from social services. Children are being taken into foster care, when individual families only ask for or need help (Support not Separation 2020).

It was an extremely difficult time, but I knew about the 1989 Children's Act and the responsibility of the social workers for the welfare of a child. I could now be articulate, and I spoke to the Director of the social services. I backed this up with full letter of complaint, with the support of Dave. Eventually there was a case review about Caitlin of which I have a copy, where Sian told the social workers she could not give Becca any money or Caitlin's child benefit, as she had to pay the bills.

In consequence, Dave's new wife offered her support after which Caitlin went to live with them for a while until she was able to return to Sian with social work support. The interesting thing was initially the social workers thought it was me who had offered the practical support instead of Dave's new wife, as I still had Dave's surname.

Sian had several episodes in hospital as she became more anxious and with paranoia, eventually she was diagnosed with border line personality disorder (See Chapter 18).

What I am trying to show is how difficult it is for some families to communicate with social services when they need help, with social services not fully investigating a case and in them making decisions without all the evidence. It has however, to be borne in mind that social workers change jobs often over time, either they move on, or up the social work ladder away from front line cases. But that should be no excuse for not listening to families and foster carers as the child's welfare is always paramount.

Chapter 14

CRISIS OF CONSCIOUS

Decisions about Social Work as a Career

In the two years post-divorce from 1986, whilst still working part time in the company, I took course in psychology and sociology. In addition, I did voluntary work with people with mental health problems, for MIND and Gingerbread for Lone parents. After leaving the company in 1988, but whilst still living in the local area, I studied and trained for four years as a counsellor, and worked with a community based counselling service. I felt not so alone by these experiences, and the skills I developed helped me with my daughters.

I finally decided to move away from the local area in 1993, primarily for my own sanity and for my daughters to get outside help without the social workers depending on me. I also decided the idea of studying social work was a way to continue to help my daughters, and to use my skills to train for a career.

My perception of social work was of case studies and supporting families, but it became obvious through my training that modern day social work was moving into crisis management. Social workers, at the time, seemed to me to make arbitrary decisions and judgements, without listening to people. Morally and ethically I was having to do things which was totally against helping, supporting, listening to, and encouraging empowerment in people, which I had been trained to do as a counsellor. I was having a crisis of conscious as I was agreeing with the clients and foster carers, and not the social workers I was working with.

The social workers who had been 'professionally' trained looked down on foster carers, yet foster carers support children 24 hours a day and know more about these children than many of the social workers. Communication between the social service departments had also been a problem whilst on placement, and two children subsequently died in a fire because of a lack of communication between the childcare team and child protection team. However, that was after I had left.

Counselling, is about listening and empowerment and is the antithesis of modern day social work. Social work is based on judgements about people, political correctness and not necessarily about the long term welfare of the child; in what may become their loving and stable home.

In 1995, it became obvious to me that I was not going to be a social worker, and for moral and ethical reasons it was time for me to leave the course: To conduct other studies or find work. Some of my tutors were very angry at my decision because of their investment, as I only had months to go before finishing the course.

One tutor, however, seeing me looking sad, came and sat by me, and then she talked to me about how she understood where my feelings stemmed from. She explained that her husband had a passion about birds which she did not share, and she saw in me a passion for people that other tutors and social workers did not share, which made sense to me. Later, I found out, through studying my family history, where that passion came from (See Chapter 15).

1995 was the year that I also decided to change my name, including my Christian name, legally by deed. I wanted to name my own inner identity which gave me strength. I no longer wanted be defined by the roles in my life, of someone's wife, ex-wife, mother of Sian or adopted children, social work student, or 'murderous' daughter in law, all associated with overwhelming guilt associated with my old name. I could now make decisions for myself.

For me I just could not continue to finish a degree course that I could not in all conscience believe in, but the tutors told me I would have to fail the whole course. I could not believe it as I had studied so hard, so I went to see an Academic advisor who made an appointment for me to see the Dean. The Dean was exceedingly helpful and said I should not have to fail the course, especially after I explained my views. So, he offered me a place to finish my degree on another related course and to act as my mentor.

The Dean offered me to study a BA Combined Degree and I studied, and completed, Anthropology and Abnormal Psychology modules. However, financially I had to leave university to get a job as my money was running out, and I did not want to get into debt. I do not know what went on behind the scene, but I left Oxford Brookes University with a Diploma in Social Work and a Diploma in Higher Education in 1996. By now all my daughters were grown up.

I am not the easiest person to be with when I feel so strongly about something which has to do with my overwhelming sense of duty, my conscience, morals and ethics. My family history explains how deep that is within me and where it came from.

Chapter 15

MY FAMILY HISTORY

Questions and Insights

What inner motivation drove me to adopt siblings from one family, and stay connected with them when others may have given up?

Experiences during my childhood and some family history background gave clues in answer to this and other questions that I had been asked, which was difficult for me to answer. My life was in the context of the time, geography, and gender expectations as a girl from a working class background, where you had to support your family.

I was born in 1950 during the early post-war years and both my parents worked, so from an early age I spent the summers and school holidays with my grandmother (my dad's mum). My grandmother was a great influence on my life and it was not until much later did I realise what a great person she was. My earliest memories was of her taking me to a centre where they distributed dried milk and fresh orange juice to expectant mothers, something the WVS did in post war centres around the UK.

At seven years old I began to see how busy life was for my paternal grandmother, yet she still remained true to the conventions of being a 1950s wife. For example, my grandmother was always home by 4 o'clock to get dinner ready for my grandfather, who was a coastal mariner; despite how busy she was during every day. Everywhere she went she took and included me, which made me feel special. On Wednesdays she would set up and open the Darby and Joan Club in the Methodist church hall, which she used to run as a WVS (Women's Voluntary Service later Royal) Volunteer leader. There was a children's chapel in the church, where my grandmother would sit with me and teach me prayers and hymns. She would then leave me in the peace and quiet, whilst she finished setting up the room and the tea urns until the other helpers arrived.

The Darby and Joan Club consisted of mostly older women who had lost their husbands, brothers, or sons, during the two world wars, and they made a fuss of me being so young. I had cuddles, biscuits and extra buns and they talked to me. I went round giving raffle tickets, and I learnt and sang with them all the old songs. These were indomitable women, but to me they were matriarchal and substitute mother figures. These women were role models to me, and this experience would explain where some of where my maternal instinct came from.

On other days my grandmother would take me see other people, those who were sick, disabled, lonely, or bereaved and anyone who could not visit the Darby and Joan club. I discovered, recently, that she also was a Deputy Leader of a Civil Centre for the armed forces and local volunteers in Newport I.O.W., during the war.

When I was 14 my grandmother presented the Queen with a bouquet of flowers during the Queen's visit to the I.O.W. in 1965. The Queen asked my grandmother about her long service in the WVS and thanked her for her 40 years of service and dedication to helping others. What I discovered was my grandmother was unanimously selected by everyone at the Darby and Joan Club to present that bouquet to the Queen.

I felt safe and loved from my experiences with my paternal grandmother different than with my own mother.

My mother's expectations of me was to stay at home to help care for my father, and eventually to care for her. Upon reflection she did not want me to have a life of my own. My mother did not want me to go on school trips, or to make friends, she did not want me to take exams, or learn to cook.

In fact my mum did not want me to do anything that would take me away from her or make me marriageable. My mother found it difficult to cope with life herself, and in caring for my father. My relationship with her was a role reversal where I became the main carer of my father. I matured early in my life and took on responsibilities that should not have been mine until I was much older. I suppose today I would be called a young carer.

Education was an anathema to my mother as she left school at the age of fourteen and only read two books in the whole of her life. She never did voluntary work, shunning the closeness of others, even though she had seven brothers and sisters. I always wanted an education. I used to secretly sneak books home as other girls of my age sneaked cigarettes. Even the school teachers did not realise they thought I just didn't read books. One teacher told me I should read books on horses and ballet (I went to a Girls school), when I was actually reading books on science, natural history, adventure and travel, at a relatively early age.

I learnt duty, responsibility, caring, empathy, conscientiousness, commitment and, supporting your husband from the early experiences with my grandmother and even from the negative experiences of my mother. I was told later by a marriage guidance counsellor that I had an overwhelming sense of duty and a class 'A' conscious. I now know where I got them from and also where I got the need to put my husband first, from all my early experiences. From post war life, gender issues of the time, the geographic area of living on an island, and the role models from my family both positive and negative.

In consequence, however, this led to a denial of self and these experiences are where the depth of my feelings came from to support my husband, to honour the commitment I made to him, especially as he had given up his mother for me. A commitment to him, where I gave up or supressed the need to have my own baby, when I found out he could not have children. This commitment extended to our daughters to keep them together throughout all the traumas.

However the need for an education remained strong within me, but remained supressed as the duality of my family experiences made me shy and subservient, where I put others need far above my own including taking continued abuse from my mother-in-law. But these experiences also made me strong where I could put my children first and dedicate myself to try and help them overcome their individual difficulties and damage.

Why did adopting three children be natural to me?

Further investigating my family history gave me clues. My paternal grandmother, mentioned above, helped to bring up the five children of my grandfather's sister as well as her own two boys. My grandmother on my mother's side had a child born out of wedlock that was brought up by my maternal Great Grandmother, as my grandmother's sister. My Great Aunt was my maternal grandmother's older sister, and she ran a home for unmarried mothers at a time when unmarried mothers were shunned by society. This Great Aunt also adopted or brought up as her own, three children with learning difficulties.

I also discovered that my two cousins lived with my mum, dad and me for a year during the first and second year of my life. My mum's brother was in the military police during the war and met his German wife just after the war, whilst stationed in Germany, and they had three children a boy and two girls. My uncle's wife subsequently met an American G.I. and left with him to go to America taking the boy with her, and leaving my uncle with the two girls. Hence my mother looked after them until my uncle got his life sorted out. So my mother looked after three girls for a while, though I cannot remember, so temporarily my cousins were my substitute siblings. Adopting three girls for me may not have been so strange after all.

Taking on other people's children must have been a subconscious motivation as I did not know any of this until well after I adopted my daughters. However, these experiences within my family history could explain why adopting children felt natural to me.

Post Script: Becca on talking to her biological mother discovered that in their family history there was pattern where their families gave away or got others to look after their children!

What made me stay committed to my adopted daughters?

Never once did I want to give up on my daughters despite the difficulties. To me they were my daughters, and I was as committed and loved them as if they were my own birth children. However, they did come with a past and I think with hindsight I was trying my best to put that right for them, which was an impossible task. This motivation was just like I had asked of myself when trying to save my dad.

During his life and time in hospital my father had always helped others just like his mother, my grandmother, so he was a role model for me too. In the times we had together during his recovery we would talk about science, nature, the universe, life, death and religion amongst other subjects, and he encouraged and validated my opinions much to my mother's disapproval. I met many people from all walks of life with him so I can talk to everyone and be articulate. This helped me through the adoption process and in asking help for my children. My father in validating my opinions and in helping me to be articulate, gave me the confidence to influence others, to setup our business, and to have confidence in my future studies, when the children had grown up.

My daughters grew up surrounded by books, are above average intelligence and they have good jobs and a chance to explore their talents. I now have two Open University degrees and I am an eternal student.

Father's influence and Parents Marriage

My dad was trying to always to do the right thing for me despite the odds and he took me everywhere. I helped him in his business and he taught me admin and business skills. My Dad and Mum's marriage was not easy as they came from so very different backgrounds. My mum came from a family of gamblers and her gambling was a constant problem in their marriage.

My dad was exceedingly intelligent, eventually becoming a Company Director. He was a well-known philatelist, known worldwide, and a fellow of the Royal Philatelic Society. But my mum left school at 14. My mother found it extremely difficult coping with my dad's lifestyle, and the serious illnesses he had, on and off, most of his life.

So, what impact did their marriage have on me that connected to my future life with my daughters?

First of all, my father taught me the value and responsibility of money through gambling. From an early age I had played cards after school with my mum and her family, and on Friday nights my father would play cards too. By nine years old I was nicknamed Maverick (for those who remember, the whiz kid, poker playing cowboy), and I could play poker with the best of them.

When I started work my father made me play with my own money, and said what you win you keep but what you lose, remains lost, so I learnt not to play unless I was willing to lose the money. Gambling became to me just the money I was willing to lose and my excitement was in how long I could play the game. Subsequently, I have always managed my money well, and I have never been in serious debt. My mother gambled all my father's money away after he died.

Post script: Becca and I had a serious clash over her debts that affected our relationship, but that comes later in the story. But now I can see where my strength of attitude comes from.

The skills I learnt from my dad in business, attitude to money and in getting expert help enabled Dave and me to set up a successful business, when he was made redundant, soon after we had officially adopted the girls. The money to set up the business came from my dad's second stamp collection that my mother gifted to me over several years.

My relationship with my mum was very different where she talked continuously about the war, her fear, anxiety, and the constant poverty their large family (she was one of eight) suffered from. I thought that was just stories growing up, but recently I found out that my mother worked in a factory making spitfires and her bus home was once strafed by a German plane. She however, was fine but it left her with continual anxiety.

My mother did not cook, my dad was the main cook in our house, and he cooked the Christmas dinner and made the Christmas cake. But my mother was very generous with her money. Though I didn't have many cooked dinners from her she would buy a box of a Mars bars, even if I wanted just one.

My daughters loved my mum, for when we were on holiday she would buy the girls' two ice creams each, they would each have two packets of their favourite cereal, and she would buy them any toys they wanted. Mum's friends and neighbours also swamped the girls' with toys from their children, and my daughters always had a pile to play with. One day my mum and her friends took Tiffany, when she was a tiny dot, to the play park whilst I took Becca and Sian around London and the Natural History Museum, and it seems we all had a good time.

It can be seen where the depth of my feelings stemmed from, my paternal Grandmother, my maternal Great Grandmother, my maternal Great Aunt, my dad and even my mum. These feelings subconsciously motivated me to cope in caring for others and in coming through all my family trauma, which made me suitable as an adoptive parent and subsequently enabled me cope with some of the behaviour of my daughters.

Chapter 16

WHERE ARE WE ALL TODAY?

Sian

In retrospect we all muddled through, Sian is still alive after all her self-destructive behaviour and does not have a criminal record. She is, however, rude to everyone, has paranoia and a borderline personality, and has been in psychiatric care a few times as an adult. Sian is unable to empathise, or see anyone else's point of view, blames everyone else for her problems, and never accepts any responsibility.

Physically her health has deteriorated over the years, she now has emphysema, carries an oxygen bottle around with her, and has one kidney all due to her lifestyle and smoking. Sian discharges herself out of hospital after arguing with the nurses and often landed on Becca's doorstep in her hospital gown. Sian also blamed a consultant for her lung disease, but he retorted with anger that it was her continued smoking that caused the lung disease. I think Becca at times found it difficult to cope with Sian's behaviour and Becca has now moved to another county. Tiffany stays in the background, and is not living close to Sian.

My relationship with Sian at this time came to an end, as I became exhausted by her behaviour over the years, and the last time we had spoken was when she, an adult, told me to fuck off as I was not her mother. I have done so and I feel relief. After everything I tried to do for her, she never apologised, was totally ungrateful, and she had disowned me, so now I do not have to have anything directly to do with her. Sian's biological mother, who is now back on the scene, also has problems with Sian's behaviour and Sian's questions about the past which her biological mum won't answer. They do not see each other very much or at all, though all three of us met up at Tiffany's wedding party in 2019, a very interesting experience, but that comes later in the story. Suffice to say Sian did speak to me about her now being a grandmother and in me being Luca's great grandmother. I now feel a warmth towards her.

Sian has two children Caitlin 26 and Layla 21 now both adults living away from home.

Sian was in a relationship about 27 years ago and thought her partner would stay around if she got pregnant by him, so she didn't tell him she had come off the pill. When she was twenty in 1994 she had Caitlin, but the father left them, as he had felt manipulated and had become a father under false pretences. However, Caitlin's father sends money and cards to her and financially helps out at times, but has not and will not take any part in her growing up. Caitlin told me she feels bereft and very angry with her father, but her story comes later too. Caitlin has grown up ok with all the support she has had over the years and now has Luca, my great-grandson.

Sian also had Layla by a different father, though Layla's father still sees her and she has been living with him and his family, he is not part of Sian's life. I however, am not familiar with Layla's behaviour, but I do fear for her as she has been brought up under Sian's influence most of her life.

Becca

Becca is married to Ryan and they have two children Courtney 21 and Callum 17, who is autistic. In 2004 my mum died and Becca got married soon after, when Callum was about 18 months old. Dave said nothing to me about my mother's death at the wedding and Scarlett, Dave's new wife, continued to be rude to me and in the presence of Mike my partner. Scarlett told Mike about my name change thinking he did not know and I could see that Mike was angry with her.

In Dave's speech he only said how Scarlett was a perfect mother and that he had brought the girls' up since the adoption, with no mention of me. That made Mike even angrier as he knew that wasn't the case. I just stared at Dave and Scarlett in utter disbelief, but I needn't have worried as the girls' school friends knew all about their past. One of Becca's friends, who also worked with Dave in the company, came up to me as said what a bitch Scarlett was. Becca's friend went on to take a photo of Becca with me and Mike.

I enjoyed Becca's wedding and she asked me to read out a beautiful poem to which I was honoured and I found it quite moving. I just felt sad overall about the wedding as to why people can't be civil to one another at a supposedly enjoyable event. Becca is now a manager within the helping professions.

Tiffany

Tiffany had Chloe, now 21, when she was in a relationship with a man with whom she had felt secure and they set up home together. However, the relationship was based on domestic abuse which Tiffany confided in me at the time, and I contacted the local police for help. Obviously Tiffany would have to report the abuse herself to the police, but I asked them to take it seriously if she did, as her partner had pushed her over and smashed her head on the patio. Tiffany did finally report the incident and left her partner. His mother was appalled by her son's behaviour and continued to support Tiffany and helped in looking after Chloe.

Tiffany is now married to a lovely guy, who I trust implicitly. Though he is much older than Tiffany they are so happy together and he is good for her. I told him I am proud to be his mother-in-law and he said likewise. Tiffany is a manager also within the helping professions but a different one to Becca.

There was a lot of sibling rivalry when my daughters became mothers, as they all became pregnant within three months of one another in 1999, as can be seen by three of my granddaughters now being 21. My daughters now live in different parts of the country.

Dave's Death and Consequences

In 2005 Dave died of cancer and I did not go to the funeral. I know the girls' were surprised I didn't go, but they did not question my motives at the time. Though I did say to Becca that I would attend the funeral to support them all if they needed me.

A few years ago I sent the girls' a letter explaining the situation, when I thought they were distancing themselves from me, and I assumed the cause was me not attending their adoptive dad's funeral. The girls' did not know about my past with Dave, with the family traumas around the marriage.

In the letter I explained to my daughters, though Dave and I were married and we adopted them I would not have gone to his funeral, if I could have helped it, as I now had a greater respect for myself and I did not have to be involved with other's disturbed behaviour. I think perhaps the girls' now understand why I did not want to attend the funeral, with Dave's mum and Scarlett being there.

I am pleased though that despite everything our daughters did have a good relationship with Dave when they were adults.

I had mentioned to Becca a few years ago that I liked the way she and her sisters' were given money, over the years, in smallish amounts from Dave's Will by Scarlett, because of Sian's demanding behaviour and to keep that pressure off her sisters.

So I got a copy of Dave's Will (a public document) as I was thinking of doing the same, when writing my Will. I got a shock when reading Dave's Last Will, his daughters were not one of main beneficiaries. The Will stipulated that Scarlett was his main beneficiary, which as his wife was understandable, but in the event of her death occurring within thirty days of Dave's death the house and 'chattels' were to go to his stepson (Scarlett's, son by from one of her two previous marriages), and the business was to go to Tim (A worker in the company who we had employed as a young man, and who had worked his way up to Director Level). Any monies remaining from Dave's estate, after debts were paid, were to be split in various sized shares between Dave's mum, his sister, his stepson and then between his daughters. I was quite angry when I read the Will because I thought that by 1999 when Dave had written the Will he would have treated the girls equally as main beneficiaries with his stepson.

However, Dave must have come to some agreement with Scarlett prior to his death in 2005, because our daughters have been getting some money from her, for birthdays, Christmases, and when they are in financial trouble. I am pleased our daughters do have a good relationship with Scarlett as any money coming to them predominantly came from the business, which I helped set up with my Dad's money! This last comment is probably a bit below the belt, but perhaps others can understand my feelings after the way I have been treated.

Chapter 17

UPDATE ON THE GIRL'S BIOLOGICAL FAMILY

The Biological Father

We, as a family, never heard about the girls' biological father whilst they we growing up until something happened by chance about 8/9 years ago? Tiffany was living with Chloe in privately rented accommodation, when her boiler ceased up and she had to call in a repair man. The man came along and spoke in an accent which sounded familiar to Tiffany and she asked where he came from. When he told her Tiffany was surprised, and she told him that she and her sisters were adopted from there, to his surprise. It appeared the boiler man was their biological uncle and he had been looking for them since 1993, to tell them their biological father had died.

It appeared that the girls' biological father had committed suicide by using a crossbow attached to the bedroom door and he died by an arrow in the eye and that this brother had found him. Subsequently, the girls made contact with the family, though Sian did not want any further contact after seeing her biological uncle.

Becca and Tiffany, subsequently visited the family and met their grandmother who had dementia. Tiffany told me she felt very uncomfortable, as perfect strangers where hugging her, and she did not have much contact with them after the visit. Becca however, continued to make contact, especially with the grandmother.

From what I understand, from all the written reports, their biological father was never criminally charged with the threats to knife the social worker, or with the threats to kidnap and kill us all. The biological father was never charged with criminal neglect of the children, as far as I know. At one stage he was living with another woman with two children and he continued to have problems.

The Biological Mother

A few years ago Sian wanted to find her biological mother and pushed Tiffany through guilt to find her for her, though Tiffany herself and Becca at the time did not want to find their mother. However, Tiffany did some research through local telephone calls, not in the hope of finding their biological mother, but to satisfy Sian that she had tried. However, their biological mother was living within the county, only half an hour travelling distance away, and was one of the responders to Tiffany's telephone calls.

Subsequently all my daughters met their mother and still have various levels of contact with her.

However, contact is a bit on and off as Tiffany keeps saying she does not know this person. Becca and her husband went on holiday with her biological mother and then boyfriend and came back saying never again. As her mother was hypercritical, and demanding of her boyfriend in public. However, Becca has made contact with extended family and relatives. Sian has distanced herself from her biological mother because she refuses to answer Sian's questions about the past.

Their biological mother told the girls she had desperately tried to find them for years and that she didn't give them up, as it was Dave and I who were pushing for the adoption. But, she has never explained why she deserted the children, permanently, when they were so young or why she left a baby. Their biological mother knew her husband was a violent man, but she still left the children with him, including Tiffany at four months old.

It was the social workers who eventually found their biological mother, living within another county, living with another man, who said he did not want anything to do with her children. I had always apologised to my daughters for their biological mum's behaviour, as I thought perhaps she had post-natal depression when she left Tiffany as a baby. I was mistaken she left all the girls' to live with another man and by the time the social workers had found her she had had his baby.

Their biological mother, since the desertion of the girls', has had a further two children by different fathers and has had several boyfriends since. Recently I found further details about their biological mother's desertion when reading more of the written files I have in my possession and when composing my response to Becca's letter, but that comes later in the story (See Chapter 20)

I had no problem, initially, when their biological mother came back on the scene, but I did feel a little strange knowing the past as I did from the reports I had received post adoption. I still felt it was important for the girls' to have contact with their biological mother, as she could answer questions I could not. I felt the girls' needed to know about their heritage, family and medical histories, for their own sake and their own children's wellbeing. However, I became uncomfortably aware that the biological mother was telling my daughters things that were not true.

The biological mother was telling the girls' that the social workers interpretation of their biological father's violent behaviour was not true. However, the police and the courts did not take the girls' into care and subsequently adopted for nothing. I also understand from Becca that their biological mother was telling them about how their father may not have committed suicide, but was murdered. It is very likely their biological father did commit suicide as he had tried it before and Sian had stopped him.

Nowhere, has it been mentioned the reasons for their biological mum leaving their biological father, and as far as I know she has never told the girls'.

I know everyone will have their own points of view about events, but I had never really told the girl's my experiences in an effort to protect them, but I realised their biological mother and certainly Dave and Scarlett had told them things about me that were not true. I have documentary evidence to support a lot of what I have been saying, and as my daughters are now adults I thought it was about time they knew the truth from my perspective. In my letter I told them if they had any questions concerning me please ask me rather than getting opinions from others, as I would answer them as honestly as I could.

I wanted my daughters to know, despite of what others are telling them, that I am proud of them. Becca and Tiffany now have loving men in their lives. I am proud of how they have brought up Chloe, Courtney and Callum and they are a credit to my daughters. I know I have missed out on being close to them and all my grandchildren because I am geographically faraway and I feel sad about that, but I wanted them to know that I love them as much now as I did when I adopted them. I feel sad for Sian and though we are estranged I still feel a deep connection to her through our shared past.

Chapter 18

MY INSIGHTS INTO THE GIRLS' BEHAVIOUR/RECENT RESEARCH

In my opinion the girls' still have behavioural problems stemming from their past. I had written this piece on my insights into their repeat patterns of behaviour before accessing new research on the consequences of attachment disorder, which I have added for clarity. This research aids my understanding into the girls' behaviour, past and present, and helps me to stop feeling guilty that I am responsible for their current problems. The research is so new which explains why help wasn't available years ago, when I adopted the children.

What is Attachment Disorder: 'Attachment Issues' is a phrase used to describe a variety of behaviours which may arise after a child has lost 'her' 'mother and has experienced emotional abandonment in early years' (Care for the family 2020).

My daughters' biological mother left them first when Tiffany was 4 months old and then she came back some months later, for two weeks, after which she abandoned them again permanently. Becca was about four and Sian about six years old when she left the final time.

According to Focus on the Family (2020) article 'every adopted child has experienced a disrupted attachment' even a pre verbal child. I had three siblings that fitted this criteria. Both sets of research list a similar array of behaviours, but I will select those that are relevant to my individual daughter's displayed behaviours.

Repeat Patterns of Behaviour

Becca

From a very young age Becca has had an over ideal view of family life. Family life and a marriage that is unrealistic to the point she has got herself into huge amounts of debt, asking for money even from other family members and friends. Becca equates love to money, so she is very materialistic, and her husband and children only have to ask for something and she tends to give it to them, whatever the cost. This makes me concerned about her children's future as they won't have everything they want when they want it, and life again will be unrealistic and future relationships difficult (See Chapter 20).

Becca's behaviour can be understood under Indiscriminate Affection behaviour, which is overly love for some people and distant or disconnected from others (Care for the Family 2020).

I never realised Becca's attitude to money or the level of her debt until quite recently, though I did know how deep she equated love and ideal family life with money. Becca did not pick up this attitude to money from me with my background, as I am careful with money (See Chapter 15). I have never been in serious debt, or even asked anyone for money. Becca often asks for money from friends and family by telling them sob stories, and does not always repay the money as promised, and sometimes she hopes people would write of the debt.

Becca's husband, however, has not worked for years, and they both have a similar attitude to money. Becca thinks her husband is absolutely wonderful and in my opinion this is an unrealistic view as no partner is absolutely perfect. I may be wrong, but my professional experience suggests that Becca has a need to control and that she is in a negative co-dependent relationship with her husband. Becca's behaviour and attitude to money makes me feel like we are being played again, so Becca can get her own way as she did when young and got the recorder from her friend, by pleading poverty.

Becca and I have recently clashed big time over her attitude to debt, as it involved me after Tiffany's wedding party (See Chapter 20). Becca's has had in the past court orders and once was nearly made bankrupt form debt, despite earning a reasonable salary. Becca's behaviour also shows that debt is a continuation of her biological father's behaviour and the dishonesty, lying and the manipulative behaviour that goes with debt. (Focus on the Family 2020).

Becca displays a lack of impulse control in her spending and a need for immediate self-gratification without thinking about the consequences of her behaviour. Again Becca displays this overly love for her husband that is unrealistic. There seems to be a need for her to control situations and her husband, which can be related to attachment problems; where the child and later the adult feels they have to be responsible for themselves, as 'no one else can be depended upon' (Focus on the Family 2020).

Tiffany

Tiffany seems a lot better and mature, but she used to have a problem with her body image and some past photos show her almost anorexic. I think this has improved and she is now happy. Tiffany has difficulty forming emotional bonds to women (mother figures) which she holds at a distance, which could have been caused by the rejection of her biological mum. Tiffany's biological father and Sian did not have the comforting chest that babies need from their mother's in the early bonding stages after birth, and as a result she probably has a greater feeling of abandonment. Tiffany, however, can respond to men, particularly older men, and her partner (now husband) is 14 years older than her. Predominantly though Tiffany was deprived of love from a mother that may have coloured her later emotional attachments to women, including me, and I don't think she was emotionally close to Scarlett either.

The research shows that Tiffany possible anorexia and body image issues placed her into the high risk group of behaviours linked to adopted children (Holden 1991). It can be seen that abandonment caused Tiffany to have difficulty with making deep emotional relationships with mother figures. No matter how much I loved her as the baby, there has always been a disconnection in our relationship, particularly as she got older where she cannot accept my love. This behaviour comes under Disinhibited Attachment Disorder (Kay et al 2016).

Tiffany did display and might have the indiscriminate affection for others, similar to Becca, but expressed differently. Tiffany displays this behaviour to strangers, as we noticed when seeing her on holiday with an older couple, whom she had briefly met on a previous holiday. Tiffany found out when and where this couple were going on holiday again and followed them without the couple knowing. Tiffany insisted to her partner they go too and arranged to go on the same plane. On the plane she hid from this couple to surprise them when they landed, which they did. Tiffany also put this couple first on one of the top tables at her wedding party above other close friends and family.

These types of behaviour of indiscriminate affection, disconnection and abandonment is called Disinhibited Attachment Disorder as this applies particularly to children adopted between 7 and 24 months. Tiffany was 21 months when I adopted her but we had already fostered her for a year (Kay, Green and Sharma, 2016).

Sian

Sian's behaviour at the time of the adoption was lying, stealing, and cheating, but it can be seen how complex her behaviour came later with the arson, joyriding and bullying.

The lack of empathy, manipulation, and the guilt she generated in others, and in her psychiatric diagnoses of borderline personality and paranoia. Sian is Sian as ever and has become more physically disabled and security conscious with her paranoia. Sian's behaviour over the years has reflected her biological father's behaviour which has been difficult to counteract, because this behaviour was established within her personality before the age of seven. Sian's past choices may have also affected Caitlin her daughter.

The research shows that there is a higher level of personality disorders in adopted children with increased levels of paranoia, anxiety and antisocial behaviour (Westermeyer et al. 2015). Sian's behaviour, past and present, consists of manipulative behaviour, lack of empathy, stealing, lying, and showing no remorse. She is demanding, attention seeking, and with a fascination for fire and horror stories. All behavioural traits associated with adopted children who experienced early childhood stress. (Focus on the Family, 2020). In addition, there is research that indicates a relationship between the fascination with fire and early sexual abuse, though other professionals and myself have suspicions that this occurred with Sian we have no direct evidence.

Caitlin

Caitlin, Sian's first daughter, now has Luca and is a good mum she also is a paediatric health assistant at a hospital. Her main problems are that Luca's father is a foreigner she met on holiday and they have been in an off/on relationship since. Cultural differences and distance are the problem, but Caitlin insisted she really loved this man and was hoping he would come to Britain for a short stay. Caitlin deeply believes that Luca must have contact with his biological father at all costs. However, this man is now being rude and abusive to Caitlin by stalking her on Facebook etc. Perhaps the pregnancy and in keeping the father in close contact are repeat behaviours of Sian's behaviour, plus Caitlin's own experience as a child with her own father.

Caitlin too seems to play on sob stories to get what she wants from people. I got a call from Becca to help with rescuing Caitlin and baby Luca from the foreign country, where Luca's father lived as he had broken up with her. So, she was left with no money and a new baby in a foreign country, so I transferred a large sum of money over to Caitlin and I was prepared to go to this country to rescue her and my great-grandson. However, the situation wasn't as dramatic as she and Becca had portrayed, as Luca's father had come back to Caitlin and she stayed with him for a few more days before flying back to Britain. As it can be seen the contact I have with my daughters is always full of angst and there is more of this later in my story.

Does this show repeat patterns of behaviour passing on through the generations?

I have learnt a lot from the research that helps me to understand, in the here and now, the past and present relationships with my daughters, that has caused me such distress over the years and makes me realise, though I tried my best, I did not get everything right. I can now forgive myself, as I obviously had no help and support from any social workers despite asking often. Both Social Services, the local social services and those where we adopted the girls', absolved themselves of any responsibility to help, and in consequence I was left with no support despite their promises.

In addition, I, in having little experience with children and in being an only child, was told I supposed to get lots of help and continuing support from social workers, from whichever the county the girls were in, but it never happened. I did not and nor did I, until very recently, discover that as an adoptive parent I should have recognised my own needs, and asked for respite care with the girls', but this has only come about by accident through divorce and co-parenting (Focus on the Family 2020).

Today, there is a Government fund given to Local Authorities for the care of adopted children, especially given to adopted parents as financial help for therapeutic assistance. In 2019, the sum was £2500 for specialist treatment, per child, per annum, and £5000 for therapy, per child, per annum. Adoptive parents would need to apply directly to their Local Authority after the child has reached 3 years of age. Information can be sought directly through the Adoption Support Fund Team (GOV.UK) or through the charity Adoption UK.

It is interesting to note, some adoptive parents do not know about this funding though they may be entitled to it. Local Authorities often do not tell adoptive parents that funding is available to them or they say funding is at Local Authority discretion.

Dave and I never had any financial or therapeutic help post adoption, even though our daughters needed the help and so did we. I suppose I have always tried to help my daughters get over their past damage to have better lives, even as adults, like the original social workers told us, and I now with hindsight can see that was an impossible task. (Focus on the Family 2020).

The research also shows that 'children with disrupted attachments may not warm to you as you may have expected. They may push you away, play one parent against another, prefer one parent and reject attempts to love them'. I have experienced these types of behaviour from all my daughters over time. (Focus on the Family 2020).

Never in 39 years have I been told, like adoptive mothers today, to look after myself over and above the children. I have only recently been able to switch off about my daughters' problems, even though they are now adults. The research suggests you 'try not to take their behaviour personally', and this has been very extremely difficult for me to do considering my past and our experiences during the marriage difficulties, business and divorce (Focus on the Family 2020)

The research also suggests my daughters' behaviour was caused by the desertion of their biological mother known as the 'woundness of the child' or as other writers suggest the 'Primary Wound' (Verrier 2020). The research, however, was mainly done on single adopted children and not on siblings within a multiple adoption, where in my case the problems were multiplied three times and collectively (Focus on the Family 2020).

I as an only child did not realise how deep or unhealthy the attachments were and are between my daughters. Which I think Tiffany suffers from most, from Sian's guilt trips to Becca's deceit, though Becca would be horrified at this. For example, Tiffany won £20,000 on an app game and she gave both her sisters £500 pound each, and was able to bring her own wedding forward which she wanted to pay for herself. Becca pleaded to Tiffany giving her a sob story, and Tiffany gave her another £1400 which Becca, now earning £68,000 per annum, promised to repay before Tiffany's wedding some months later. Tiffany's wedding was in October and Becca by September had only paid back £100.

Talking to Becca, I found her to be jealous of her sister. Becca still had not paid Tiffany back by the time of Tiffany's wedding party in November 2019, and I got caught up in this, because I loaned Tiffany a £1000 to cover some of what Becca owed her. But this in what I thought was a helpful decision backfired on me later in my relationships with both Becca and Tiffany (See Chapter 20).

This jealousy was evident too from Sian's past behaviour with her sisters that continued throughout childhood. Tiffany and Becca have their birthdays close together so Sian would always do something to attention seek, including threatening suicide. I can see now that Becca has the same jealousy trait with Tiffany's win. Becca promised to repay Tiffany before her wedding, but just hasn't tried. When talking to Becca previously about Tiffany's win she said 'if she can win so can I' in a very ardent tone of voice.

The research shows that jealousy can be normal amongst siblings. However, the research also shows that adoptees like Becca, with her lack of impulse control, immediate need for self-gratification and indiscriminate affection, links her present behaviour to early childhood stress. (Focus on the Family 2020).

Chapter 19

TIFANNY'S WEDDING PARTY/MEETING THE BIOLOGICAL MOTHER

Tiffany got married in Mauritius in October 2019 and held a wedding party in November 2019, when I met their biological mum for the first time and some of the girls' new relatives with whom they have become friends with. Tiffany was quick to tell me that Scarlett, their step mother, would not be attending. I think we all underestimated our feelings at that time!

The stress over the years had an impact on my health and gradually changed my feelings to helping the girls' as they got older. Up to then I thought I was doing the right thing, but in reality not. This resulted in a blow up between Becca, Tiffany and myself, post Tiffany's wedding party, post November, and in meeting the biological mother.

Prelude to the Wedding Party.

I was not worried at the time when the girls' biological mother came on the scene, when Tiffany found her by chance, after the instigation from Sian. I knew the girl's would want to know about their identity, their family

history and heritage, and health background for themselves
and their families. I knew that their biological mother had
her own perspective for giving them up, but I sincerely felt
she would tell some of the truth about the adoption. I
believed the social workers when they said that their mother
wanted the girls' to have a better life. In consequence, I did
not say anything negatively to my daughters' about their
biological mother, until after Tiffany's wedding party in
November 2019, when feelings came to a head.

Until then I had been coping or helping with the girls'
problems and the continual angst much to the detriment of
my health. In 2016, when on holiday, I had viral meningitis
and I had to spend time in a London Hospital; it took me
nine months to recover. This was followed in 2018, with the
discovery of two genetic functional bowel conditions,
inherited from my grandmother and father. In 2019, I had
an autoimmune response to a gastroenteritis infection which
gave me reactive arthritis. Not once did my daughters'
telephone or ask me how I was, and they haven't visited me
for years, though I have been visiting them.

I suddenly realised that I had been making a mistake by
putting my daughters' first all these years, physically or
emotionally, as it had been making them rather selfish. I

was until recently putting them first, though they are now in their forties.

Tiffany's Wedding Party/Consequences of Meeting the Biological Mother

I did not know until just before the wedding party in November 2019 that the biological mother was going to be there, and though that filled me a little with anxiety I decided to relax about the occasion, and to be polite to everyone. That was until Tiffany phoned me the day before the party to ask me if I wanted to sit with all the family and the biological mother, or sit with the oldies i.e. the groom's parents. I just said I would sit with Steve's parents, but my anxiety was increasing.

I did talk to some of my friends, who are mothers, to see if my anxiety was natural. They said my feelings were totally natural, considering I knew the girls past, and about their biological mother deserting them when young, and deserting a baby. Their responses were often stronger than mine, they could not believe that the biological mother would have been asked to go to the wedding party.

These mothers also felt she should not attend the wedding party, knowing I was going to be attending the too. Especially when she knew, as she did, that she had deserted the girls' twice and left them and the baby with a violent and neglectful father. Other mothers said they would not have remained quiet, one wanted a fight her, another said my daughters had no respect for me after all I had done for them, and others just gasped in disbelief.

At the wedding party I felt I was an afterthought and a little upset at the way Tiffany treated me, but nevertheless I went and overall I had a good time. I did not speak to their biological mother though I could see her and she was watching me. But I was really upset by the fact that all the family, including the grandchildren, sat with her. Mike my partner was really angry for me, as he thought I was being completely ignored.

In December I was still ill and simmering with anger and resentment, at the way I had been treated at the wedding party, but not knowing what to do about these feelings. However, when I contacted Tiffany about the money she promised to pay me back I discovered she could not, as Becca had still not paid her back. It also appeared that Tiffany had not told Steve about the loan, even though she had promised me she would. In addition, she still asked me to keep the loan a secret from Becca for fear of upsetting her. Now I wanted to find out why, but Tiffany would not say.

Meanwhile Becca phoned me to say her biological mother had told her more about the adoption; that we as adoptive parents had pushed her into signing the papers, and that we were involved in taking the girl's away from her. I reiterated to Becca that we knew nothing about their biological mother being found, or her signing the consent papers until months later when the social workers told us (which I can confirm, as I have got the social work reports). Becca did not believe me and said 'it's a matter of opinion'. When I asked why she believed her biological mother over me Becca replied 'she gave birth to us'. I was shocked!

I became suspicious, during this telephone call that Becca did have a hold over Tiffany. So I asked Becca: Who planned and decided that their biological mother was to attend Tiffany's wedding party, and where the family was to sit? Becca's response 'Tiffany is entitled to invite whom she wants' said with anger. I was confused and asked myself: What is going on here?

To say that I was livid was an understatement, I could not no longer cope with the biological mum telling lies or in keeping the girls' secrets (nor did I want too). So, in anger, I wrote a letter to the girls', and gave a copy to Mike, my partner, who was still angry at how the family had treated me at the wedding party. I also sent a copy to Steve, who was Tiffany's new husband, as I just wanted everything to be out in the open and to be honest. I could not cope any more as I was still recovering from reactive arthritis.

Maybe with hindsight sending a letter and copies in anger was not the most appropriate thing to do. But the consequences of keeping silent and protecting the girls', over the years, and coping with their behaviour, now they were adults, overwhelmed me.

My letter was followed by a letter from Becca full of hate and anger and stories from the past that were not true. All of this had surprised me considering I had the closest relationship with Becca out of all the girls. I had seen Courtney being born and had been to Becca's Graduation and her wedding, though that was a bit strained by Dave and Scarlett's behaviour, but nothing more. And Becca had told me at the time she had first contact with her biological mother that I was always going to be her Mum!

Emotional distance from Becca was created by the appearance and her continued connection with the biological mother. I did not worry about this, as I thought it was understandable, but not the hate and anger that was aimed at me, nor that I was somehow involved in taking her away from her biological mother.

All of this may have been avoided if I had more help in the past and had more understanding as to what was happening, for example, from what is now known as a 'Life Story Book' with each adopted child (Support Not Separation, 2020). A Life Story Book, from my understanding, is the information built up with each adopted child, from birth through childhood and continues to help them understand their past, to put it in perspective. It should be completed under social workers supervision.

Under normal circumstances my daughters' would also have had individual counselling help, as is usual in the case with adoptees first meeting their biological mother (Family Action, 2020). I am still not sure how this would work in a multiple adoption of siblings from one family. I also, cannot find any help on an adoptive mum's first meeting with their daughters' biological mother. I can only tell you what happened after the Wedding Party, where there was a first meeting between me and my daughters' biological mother.

Becca's letter to me was 'selective and disjointed' which may have shown her level of heated emotion. So I tried to answer her letter in the order which she had written, and therefore may contain some repetition, but I added my thoughts in the light of recent research hopefully for clarity.

Chapter 20

RESPONSE TO BECCA'S LETTER

So what follows is my response to Becca's letter, clarifies what happened, and how I felt. I also sent her an actual copy of the adoption case, showing her that the biological mother had deserted them twice, and I sent a copy to Tiffany.

Crisis

Hi Becca,

I am going to try and answer your responses to my letter as full and honestly as possible, so we can see and both understand where each of us is coming from.

Let me begin by telling you I did send personal birthday messages to Courtney, Callum, Caitlin, Chloe and Luca on their birthdays, and have never forgot them. I sent a message to Courtney on her 21st, and I got a lovely reply, that she loves us loads and hope to see us soon. She even sent me photos of her new flat! It seems that I have more contact with them than you do! Please check your facts next time Becca before trying to upset me. I am appalled with you, that you would think that I would involve the grandchildren at all.

Of course I never talked to the grand-children or involved them in my quarrel with Becca. Becca's letter was full of hate that I had actually done it.

Now back to your responses, so we can see if there is a way forward for us which I hope there will be.

Why would I want you and Tiffany to fall out? It would be the last thing I would do.

I just wanted to know what was going on between the two girls as it involved me and I was so ill at the time. Tiffany had been concerned about upsetting Becca since April 2019 and I still don't know why!

I know you are angry Becca as I would have been if I got my letter out of the blue, but I want to explain what happened and why I could not let you know.

Back in April last year, at a dinner with Tiffany and Steve, Steve told Mike that Tiffany had lent you money and he wasn't too happy. Meanwhile, Tiffany was telling me that she had given you and Sian five hundred pounds each out of her £20 thousand pound winnings, which I thought was very kind of her. However, she went on to say that she had lent you total of £1400 and that you had promised to pay it back before her wedding. But I was not to tell you that she had told me, otherwise you would be upset and never speak to her again. I agreed, I didn't think anything of it as was between the three of you, you were going to pay it back prior to the wedding. But you didn't Becca, and it was before I knew full extent about your debt.

The girl's usually told me about their sisters' behaviour if they felt I needed to know, mainly for me to do something about it, but this situation seemed different. Becca had not told Tiffany that she already owned me two hundred pounds, or that Scarlett (Stepmother) had already given her £3500. So this quite naturally raised my curiosity. Becca did not tell me about her debt to Tiffany, but did confide to me some of the level of debt she now owed people; Suffice to say it was around £11,000 without what she owed Tiffany.

Becca explained in her letter to me that she was a victim of circumstance, which wasn't true and part of the debt was due to gambling. Becca was earning £68,000 salary at this time and she wasn't living within her means, so it can be seen there was a level of deceit, dishonesty and manipulation within her relationships with family and may be others (Possible Attachment Issues?).

So what follows is what I actually put in the letter I sent in reply to hers.

People could see that you Becca and Ryan had extravagant spending long before I knew the extent of your debt darling, from seeing your two BMWs parked in your driveway, and much later from your Facebook photos. For example, of the NY car for Callum's prom, and it was evident you both liked luxury cars and lifestyle etc.

Last year when you and I discussed about your debt problems, I could see how you were living way beyond your means, and in having to pay a lot of additional money, in interest payments, on loans. However, you still did not mention to me the money you owed Tiffany, though I knew all about it, so I kept both yours and Tiffany's secrets. I have not discussed your level of debt in full with anyone, not even Mike, and especially not strangers.

By being honest and putting this to Becca she thought, and accused me of talking to strangers about her personally, but of course I hadn't. It can be seen in these above paragraphs issues of self-gratification and indiscriminate affection.

Tiffany told me prior to her wedding party she did not have enough money to cover it, as you had not paid her back in full. By this time I wasn't surprised, I knew you could not pay her back because of your level of debt, and because you still owed me £200 that I had expected back Sept/Oct, after you paid off the car loans. I offered Tiffany to loan her a £1000 so she did not have to worry anymore, and she promised me she would tell Steve, but she didn't. Tiffany promised to pay me back in full after the party, but when we talked later it was obvious she didn't have the money from you.

So I offered to take your loan off her, so you Becca would owe me instead. I offered so Tiffany could concentrate on her new marriage and prevent any upset with Steve over your debt to her. I only asked her what she thought of my suggestion and Tiffany went ballistic at me. I have repeated Facebook text messages where she was so upset at the thought of you knowing, that she had told me about your debt to her.

I tried talking to Tiffany on the phone but never got a word in edgeways, she was screaming at me that I mustn't tell you, or you would never talk to her again. I just put the phone down, as I was too unwell to listen to it all, and I just could not understand what the problem was between you two. Steve eventually phoned back and spoke to Mike and said that Tiffany was upset that I had called her a petulant child, I did not call her anything, and petulant child is not in my vocabulary. This made me more confused and upset.

I still to this day do not understand what was going on between the two of them, nor Tiffany's behaviour towards me, as I was only offering to help.

No-one talks to me like that with so much anger when I was offering to help. Tiffany's reaction suggested that you Becca had some kind of hold over her. Up to then I had kept both your secrets, but your debt to her was no longer just between you and Tiffany; it now involved Steve, Mike, and especially me.

Hence, I cannot understand and still don't understand what is going on between you Becca and Tiffany. It is interesting that Tiffany would rather upset me, but she had never been that angry me before, she was shouting that she did not want to upset you (Why?), as proved by my Facebook messages I still have. However, Tiffany told you Becca that I was the problem, and she told Steve, that what upset her most was me calling her a petulant child, which I didn't.

I have no idea Becca what is going on. I was so ill and stressed that my consultant, GP, physiotherapist, and Mike were concerned for my health, as the stress was causing parts of my body to swell and delay my recovery from reactive arthritis.

By the way I had had this condition since April and not once did you or Tiffany phone to see how I was. In fact Tiffany has never phoned me, only texted when she needed help.

This lack of contact from them had continued for several years on and off especially from Tiffany, and looking back it suggests a continuing disconnection between us, or her response to her continuing feelings of abandonment. Which I certainly wasn't aware of. Tiffany's reaction to me was an explosion of suppressed anger, which was totally over the top from the situation we were in.

The Drs and Mike told me to lessen the stress and the only way I could was to bring everything out in the open, and pushback the responsibility onto the people involved. For my daughters to take on their own responsibilities for the debt and the consequences that it has caused in all our family relationships. You can see Becca the debt was not just between you and your sister, nor should it have been in the first place. Marriage partners should come first before sisters, so Steve at least should have known everything from the very beginning.

I could not give you any warning Becca, because I did not know what was going on between you and Tiffany. It was not fair on me that your debt to her and non-payment, and in both of you not keeping your promises were the causes of Tiffany's reaction to me, when I was only offering to be helpful, so why should I keep your secrets anymore!

My daughters', are all in their forties and I think though they were damaged as children they ought to take more responsibility for themselves as adults. My mistake was I had not been treating them like adults, and I had been continually trying to help them when they told me they were in difficulty, instead of encouraging them to help themselves. I suppose wanting to help your children is a natural reaction from most parents when they see their children in trouble.

My letter continues, it can be seen in the light of research that some of the problems can be related to attachment issues, as previously mentioned.

DEBT

When Steve discovered about my loan he promised to pay me back in full the £1000 in February. Tiffany sent me, in February, a thank you card with the cheque paid in full. This is a good lesson for you Becca, as you should not ask for money unless you can pay it back in the promised time given.

Your level of debt was so high, I knew that you must have known, that you could not have paid back your loan to Tiffany by her wedding. You did not have the right to ask Tiffany for any money, in fact as sisters you should have paid her some money as a wedding present, if you had wanted her to have such a good time! I knew you were jealous of her win when during a telephone conversation with you, I said how good it was and your reply was 'if she can win so can I', said in such an ardent voice that either showed jealousy or sibling rivalry; certainly not the happiness you claim for her.

I was also aware talking to Tiffany that you, in trying to get a loan from her, were not entirely honest about your reasons, and created sob stories for wanting the loan. I have experienced that from you too darling, and though you may not want to hear it, this is manipulative, deceitful and dishonest behaviour.

Darling you are not a victim of your finances, especially now you are earning £68,000 per annum and certainly with that amount of cash coming in after costs, which is more than Tiffany's and Steve's combined salary. A lot of your immense financial pressures are of your own making and by your own admission, in not budgeting and not living within your means.

Ryan not working isn't helpful either, to his avoidance of work, lifestyle choice, or depression where he needs counselling etc. I as a professional saw all of these behaviours within the long term unemployed I worked with for years. Most unemployed returned to work, including those with disabilities, mental health problems, and those recovering from the grief of redundancy. Ryan seems reluctant to get help which is unfortunate.

I am not sure if this is a negative co-dependent relationship, as Becca likes being in total control of money, decisions about where to work, where to live and where to move too, whilst professing they have such a wonderful, perfect marriage.

Becca you are not and have not been living within yours means for a long time and it is obvious that you are now living well beyond your means. You may not be aware, but you seem to have a sense of entitlement to luxury cars and things bought on the spur of the moment etc. Becca, darling, you do not any savings to help you serve the lifestyle that you really want. I am not being deliberately horrible to you this is the reality of your situation, that I cannot be held responsible for.

I did listen, I was supportive of you and I love you lots, but I don't like the level of debt you are now in, or that I got wrapped up in your debt to Tiffany. I try to be supportive to you and Tiffany but I don't like being caught up in the secrets between you, promises you both don't keep, or the consequence of your behaviour, especially now you are adults. I am not against you or think so little of you per se.

I do not think you are a terrible person darling, just a misguided one at times, and that does not stop me loving you. You can love someone and not like some of their behaviour!

The girls' when young had no real difficulty in accepting my love. Tiffany originally used to put tissues down my top to make my chest flat, like her sister and her biological father, but later she accepted my motherly cuddles. Tiffany, when she could not speak used to have severe temper tantrums when going to bed, but eventually when I snuggled her in bed and kissed her goodnight she spontaneously said 'I love you mummy'. Becca loved hugs especially when she was upset about her biological mother leaving her, and I used to cuddle her, as I felt her loss.

However, since their biological mother came on the scene there has been very little warmth, affection, or even respect towards me, from either of my daughters, as I had when they were younger and we had a lot fun.

It seems hate and anger has taken over, either by their experiences growing up within the difficult situations of divorce, the consequences of Sian's behaviour, or in me keeping silent over the years in trying to protect them. I have notice this distancing more since the biological mother came back into their lives, but I certainly did not expect all this hate and anger.

Biological Mother

I did talk to other mothers about the appearance of your biological mother to check my feelings. You must realise that I did not know who invited your biological mother to the wedding party or where the family were to sit, I was just asked as an afterthought by Tiffany. Mike was cross because all the family was sitting with her and none spent time with me, though there was plenty of opportunity, giving the impression that I was being ignored by you all. I know you came to see me and talk about your biological mother, but I refused as Tiffany's wedding party was not the time or place for such a discussion.

Remember this was after you 'did' say that 'we as adoptive parents did push for the adoption', and that implied we took you away from her. When I questioned you at the time you did say to me 'it was a matter of opinion'; Mike can confirm this because I told him straight after you said that to me, and 'I was hurt and livid'. I did not get your comment completely wrong at all Becca and you know it!

I could not understand as Becca is a manager within the helping professions, and she knows that adoption is not just between the adoptive parents and the biological mother. I felt there was an angry child in her somewhere aimed at me.

I did talk to one friend, whose mother had left her and her sisters when young, just to try and make some sense of the situation I was in. Her mother had left them temporarily, and returned to be their mother, but it had left a scar. This friend was the one who told me that your biological mother had no right to attend family functions, after she signed the consent papers. All comments in the letter were from other mothers who I sought advice from. It seems that no-one would have adopted three of you, or put up with what I believed was your biological mother's comments. None of the mums I spoke too would have left their children so

young, and neither would you Becca have ever left
Courtney or Cameron, or Tiffany leave Chloe.

Try and see it from my perspective, your comments, along
with all the family, at the party, sat with your biological
mum, seemingly having little contact with me; or no prior
telephone discussions about the biological mum being
present, certainly made me feel ignored and neglected. It
certainly felt like I was being pushed out, by your
relationship you now have with your biological mother.
Why did you not phone me prior to the wedding party or
even after, to say you were uneasy at the time? We could
have talked about it with maturity and some understanding.

I am beginning to feel that since her biological mother's
return, Becca is splitting us into good and bad 'mother' and
I am becoming the 'bad' mother. I am still not sure what
impact this is having on Tiffany, but the situation must
being messing with I her mind too! At the wedding party
Steve told me that Tiffany would not let him be involved in
any planning of the wedding, or the wedding party, and not
to pay for anything. Steve thought it was great, but I was
suspicious about Tiffany's need for total control (See
Disinhibited Attachment Disorder, Chapter 22).

This need for control might explain Tiffany's over reaction to me, as she was screaming at me down the phone that she would rather get a pay day loan than for me to talk to Becca or for Steve to know!

Chapter 21

MY RESPONSE TO BECCA'S LETTER CONTINUES

I am not worried so much about how geographically close you are to your biological mother or your stepmother, but how close Becca, you are to them both emotionally over me, when you do not phone me at all, or very often to see how I am. I don't think darling you know anything about me, my health or my interests etc. It seems our phone calls are about angst, I am always trying to help you get a better life, but I'm now accused of interfering in your adult lives. It is as if our previous lives together and the fun we had when you were younger, prior to the arrival of Scarlett and your biological mum, no longer exists or means nothing to you or Tiffany.

So let us some clarity!

I can only go by what you say to me, as I do not know what your biological mother actually says to you, but have you thought she might want to paint herself in a better light, and give you what you want to hear, through the guilt of signing the consent papers. Let us have some reality here, your biological mother could have easily got help and support to look after you herself, if not the first time she left you but perhaps, some months later when she went back to you and saw the state you were in; she could have taken you with her the second time she left. Your biological mother left you, and later permanently gave you up for a man who did not want you, and she had his baby by the time the social workers found her.

I would have found this difficult to accept, if I was in Becca's position, if my mother had left me and had another baby by another man. But Becca still believes her biological mother's explanations. The girls' have never discussed the adoption with me.

Your dad and I fostered you all for a year with the expectation you might go back to your biological mother, if she could be found. I cannot be held responsible for what the social workers said to her, or the decisions of the court, or all the legal professionals, or that she signed the adoption papers. Becca, as a professional, within the helping professions, you are familiar with how the system works. Perhaps darling you need to think before you speak about the implications of what you say, or at least ask me questions about the adoption!

No you cannot be held responsible for being damaged children, nor can I for the damage you experienced prior to me having you. I have been trying to cope for years with the consequences of your behaviour, from the decisions that your biological mother and father made. You know I have done nothing but try to be a supportive and loving mum to you all, despite all the challenges I have experienced from you, your sisters, your dad, Scarlett, and your biological mother. I did not have the family life I had hoped for, but I fought to keep you all together, as you grew up. I do not expect a thank you from you all, but I do expect respect and some consideration.

I think today there is an emphasis on adoptive parents working with social work support for helping adopted children come to terms with their past, as no-one can possibly make up for the previous damage caused to children. My task was an onerous one without any support and within a multiple adoption.

I, over the years Becca, never had follow up social work support, or access to any help with you all, and have tried my best. In 1986, your dad did not like me divorcing him and getting it on the grounds of his unreasonable behaviour (which is a court document). Your dad wanted me to have sole custody of you all, and have to pay no money to me or for you.

You know that it would have been impossible for me to look after you all on my own, especially with all your challenging behaviour. The solicitors explained to your dad that one or all of you would have to go back into care, if he did not support me; so your dad agreed to co-parent you, as he did not want to appear a failure to anyone. The co-parenting arrangement was a legal document signed off by a Judge, and I carried on working in the company.

Two years later Scarlett was on the scene and your dad really wanted me out of the business. In 1988, my situation within the company became untenable, and I agreed I would leave the company, but with certain conditions. A clean break for me, child maintenance paid through the company for you, and that the company should continue to keep all the staff employed.

Your dad did not want to give in on any of those conditions, and said to me I would never see Sian again (She was living with him at the time) unless I signed the business over to him. I eventually taped this blackmail, which was enough proof for me to get all my conditions granted. This was supported by two solicitors, a bank manager, a tax consultant, and a legal document of which I still have. All this was happening during your and Sian's difficult teenage behaviour. How would you have coped Becca if you were in my shoes? I tried to protect you and did my best for you. Where others might have given up, I didn't.

I do not talk to strangers, as you think, but to Mike, friends and professionals to get the help and support when I needed it, and I am not going to apologise for that Becca.

There was an expectation in Becca's letter that I was the one who was to blame for everything, and I was the one who had to apologise. Of course this is unrealistic. All I wanted was good communication between us.

Reality check Becca you were born in 1975, I left for Oxford in 1993, when you were almost 18, and Tiffany was almost 14. When I left everything was done with the help of Family Conciliation, and with Tiffany's consent, as I gave her the opportunity to live with me in Oxford. It was decided between Dave, Tiffany and myself that we would have a long-distance co-parenting arrangement, supported by Family Conciliation and the court.

I can now see this decision reinforced Tiffany's feeling of abandonment, especially by my move, and encouraged by the negative comments from the family.

I did not kick you out at the age of thirteen Becca nor did I say those things to you. Sian was threatening to influence you and kidnap Tiffany, at the time, when she was living in a flat. Your dad was a co-parent and had responsibilities to help me protect your health and welfare, not someone I dumped you on. The Family Conciliation team thought it would be a good idea to split you two up for a while, and you went to live with your dad with his full consent to Family Conciliation, whilst I tried to protect Tiffany everyday as then I had the time.

This looks like miscommunication between siblings and false memories.

Your dad was upset with me because I divorced him, I got the business settled, he had to be a co-parent, and Scarlett had to look after you, and I moved away. Your dad and Scarlett didn't want me move away because I was the first port of call for the social workers and police regarding all your behaviours, especially Sian's. We did work hard though to keep you and Tiffany away from Sian's influence, to keep you both safe, and at school, so you could be the best you could be, but it didn't entirely happen that way did it Becca.

I have tried over the years to protect you from everything, but obviously I didn't see what was happening with your dad and Scarlett's unhelpful comments to you all: But, I had the full backing of solicitors, professionals, and the court in trying my best for you and your sisters, and I am not going to apologise for that either darling.

Perhaps keeping quiet and protecting my daughters over the years, and as adults, was not a good idea, but I really did not know how to handle the situation, with abused and neglected siblings within a multiple adoption. I was just, rightly or wrongly, trying to be the best mum I could be under the circumstances.

I don't want to talk or keep referring to the past either. I want us to have conversations in the here and now, but you must understand that the return of your biological mother, and your and Tiffany's behaviour towards me only makes sense in relation to the past. It seems to me that you and Tiffany have some anger towards me, which I do not understand and am trying to make sense of. Neither of you talk to me, telephone me nor ask me questions, so what am I to make of it! You accuse me of things I don't do, you don't ask questions to give me a chance to answer and Tiffany seems to have disowned me. I don't know where I am anymore with you or Tiffany.

I want to talk to you about photography, holidays, landscapes, crafts, past school friends etc. To Tiffany I want to talk about volcanoes, books, music and exercise etc. like we used too. I want to tell you that I like to study, and I'm currently learning the guitar; I have been taking art classes and I like antiques. I don't' want to talk about the past, or debts, or angst. My health is back to normal and I want to keep it that way. I would like us to have contact, but it is up to you, I am not perfect Becca, I have done my best as a mum and if it is not enough I can't do any more.

Love Mum xxx.

Post Script.

I have not heard from Becca or Tiffany since this this letter. Tiffany through Steve said she wanted to keep the past in the past, but I am not sure where that leaves me. I haven't contacted them either, though their birthdays are coming up soon, I will of course send them birthday cards, then we can see what happens.

I sent them both birthday cards, but I have had no contact. I decided to remove Becca as a friend on Facebook, much to her surprise. I think she needs time to work out her relationship with her biological mother, rather than focus all her attention on me. Tiffany still has had no contact with me, and not on my birthday either. Becca did sent me birthday card, on time too, and has become a friend again with me on Facebook, but still we don't have any direct contact.

Perhaps an update summary of the girls' behaviour, in the light of recent research, will help me to clarify and understand what is going, on enabling me to put everything in perspective.

Chapter 22

SUMMARY OF GIRLS' BEHAVIOUR

There is evidence displayed in all the children of rejection behaviour, both as young children and as adults, as evidenced by research called Rejection Theory (Adoption UK). Where adopted children push adoptive parents to the limits to reject them, in the same way as their biological mother had early in their childhood, and they continue to resist affection on parental terms.

All the girls, at one time or another, have these displayed traits under Reactive Attachment Disorder.

Becca and Tiffany, particularly displayed behavioural traits of Reactive Attachment Disorder in lying, manipulative behaviour, and in forming indiscriminate affection relationships with partners, and in Tiffany's case also with strangers. Becca when young had incessant chatter and was, particularly, very clingy. I could not go to the toilet with her wanting to come too. Perhaps this behaviour showed her fear of Abandonment. (Focus on the Family 2020).

Update: Tiffany and Steve have ended their marriage after a year. Steve cannot understand Tiffany's 'all or nothing attitude' and the finality in Tiffany's response after 8 years of lovingly being together. (See below Disconnection)

Additional Reactive Attachment Disorder traits can be evidenced, especially in Sian's behaviour; with a lack of conscience or lack of remorse, destructive behaviour to self, to others, and to property, in repeated suicide attempts, bullying, and her links to arson. Perhaps the fascination with fire could link to her experience of possible sexual abuse. In addition, she lacked the ability to empathise (Focus on the Family 2020).

Sian has a personality disorder that can be linked to adoption in histrionic, antisocial, avoidant and paranoid behavioural traits, as can be in the research on Adopted Adults (Westermeyer et al 2015).

Tiffany showed behavioural traits, particularly, under Disinhibited Attachment Disorder (Kay et al 2020) in her relationships with mother figures and in her behaviour displayed as indiscriminate friendliness to strangers, particularly when as an adult. So, too when as a very young child she displayed zombie like behaviour, and did not smile or talk. These behaviours are evidenced, more profoundly, in children adopted between 7 and 24 months and Tiffany was 20 months, from the time we fostered her.

The research also shows that relationship difficulties identified in older children is linked to the age the children were at the time of their Adoption. As my daughters were under seven at the time of our adoption they all fit into this category, linked to Disinhibited Attachment Disorder (Kay et al 2020).

All the girls' at one time or another have shown a Disconnection with us as Adoptive parents and all have displayed behaviour relevant to Abandonment in early childhood (Care for the Family, 2020). In this research it also stresses that normal parenting strategies do not work and that Adopted parents face unique emotional challenges, of which they should get help and support.

Update: Tiffany has for the last year totally disconnected from me and now her husband Steve. There is no discussion or compromise when Tiffany makes her mind up and she does not think or apparently care about how others feel. This seems to be a pattern related to the past either in early abandonment prior to the adoption and/or aggravated by the events and consequences of her relationships with her sisters.

The consequences on the girls' physical health too, is important to remember. The girls were starved and all suffered malnutrition before entering care.

Tiffany had rickets and suspected scoliosis of the spine, which she recovered from quite quickly, but she did show signs of Anorexia and body image issues in later life; though this could have had a psychological rather than a physical cause. Malnutrition had an effect on Becca as it stopped her growth, which caused her stress over her life, as she did not like being so small. The malnutrition Becca suffered from also caused Hypoplasia on her teeth, where her teeth had no enamel, and in consequence she had to have extensive dentistry on her teeth overtime. In addition, she has been diagnosed with Fibromyalgia, as an adult, which research shows is a higher risk in adults who have experienced early childhood stress (Arsivi 2015).

Sian recovered from her early malnutrition, but because of her destructive lifestyle, over the years, now has one Kidney and has Emphysema where she requires and oxygen bottle.

I am not sure, with hindsight, that having the reports about the girl's and all the information the social workers gave us was the right thing for us. It coloured my relationships with my daughters, as I knew their background and tried until recently to keep it secret, whilst trying to have close and loving relationship with them as a parent. Now the girls' just don't believe me on anything, despite me having the reports, and the court documents and in showing them now they are adults.

The girls' biological mother gives the impression there was a conspiracy at the time of the adoption of which we as adoptive parents were involved. The biological mother also says that everything the social workers and police reported about their biological father's violent and neglectful behaviour was not true, and Becca in particular believes her. But the girls' were not adopted for nothing!

Usually there is professional input and a process for adopted children to find their biological mother and for birth mothers to find their children (Family Action, 2020). The Department of Health also have produced booklets on the Adoption Contact Register and Access to Birth Records. In our case the Girls' found their own biological parents, by chance, with confused and negative consequences.

Details about their biological father was found by accident when a boiler man went into Tiffany's house to fix the boiler, and they got chatting and Tiffany found out that he was her biological uncle. It was he who told her about the death of her biological father in 1993. Sian pushed Tiffany in to trying to find their mother a few years back, by getting her to phone all the appropriate names in the area. Tiffany was not expecting to find their biological mother but she did: the biological mother was living within half an hour travelling distance from the girls' houses'.

Then the contact happened with the girls' and that is when the biological mother said she had tried for years to find them; and that she was pushed by the social workers and the adoptive parents to sign the papers. Becca is closest to her biological mother and believes her. I think Sian is not happy with her biological mother because she will not answer Sian's questions about the past and Tiffany is indifferent to her, but contact is led by both her older sisters.

To create a Life Story Book for each of my daughters was impossible for me, as I did not know about it until recently. The girl's did not ask me anything about their past and just told each other stories from their past memories, which were false considering their ages. These are the complications of a multiple adoption. None of the girls have got professional help, specifically with their adoption, as far as I know, and certainly not around contact with the biological mother. To Tiffany, in particular, it is like the past never happened. My daughters', now they are adults, think that Dave was wonderful and Scarlett's home is their second home.

Even Courtney has an elaborate tattoo of Dave, her grandfather, much to the approval of Becca. Is this a repeat of indiscriminate affection, or overly affectionate relationships similar to Becca?

There is plenty of help for adoptees and even biological/birth parents but very little for adoptive parents, who need the access to social workers and professional help as they are the ones caring for disturbed children. I found that protecting your children is just not enough! However, for me I now have some understanding of what has happened, in the light of new evidence, and I can continue living with myself without any guilt, and get on with my life.

Hindsight/What should or shouldn't have happened.

For the Girls'

I am not sure whether or not we would have adopted three siblings, who came up as an emergency, having had little experience of children ourselves.

The social workers told us, they would not have put children who had been through trauma to parents who had not come through trauma themselves, but Dave had not come to terms with his past trauma with his mother.

Dave should have had a psychiatric appraisal like I had too, and he certainly should have been honest.

I should have questioned why I had to have a psychiatric appraisal and not Dave; for he hadn't come through his family traumas. This left me coping with additional life changing experiences, like divorce, running a business, and with the continual and extra stress, over the years, without any social work support.

We should have had social work support and access to professional help from the beginning and through our lives, for the girls' and for ourselves.

We should have had professional and special therapeutic help for Sian. Even if that meant separating her from her siblings for a while.

For Myself

I should have considered myself more in all of this. I should have stood up to Dave's mother, and sooner to the emotional abuse Dave gave me.

I should have looked after my own needs and had respite, as the research suggests, because of the consequence on my health and the huge psychological stress I was under for many years.

But I survived and I have got a huge family

Chapter 23

WHAT ABOUT MY LIFE AS AN ADOPTIVE MUM
/WHERE AM I NOW

I am a Survivor and I have been lucky to have had a life of my own, after the children had grown up.

In 1996, after receiving my Diploma in Social Work and with my counselling qualification and business experience I left Oxford, and moved into rented accommodation in Windsor, to search for work in London whilst still visiting the girls. I eventually found a job in London and I became a LifeWorks Consultant, offering a helpline service for employees of large corporate companies in London, a job I enjoyed with career prospects. I was able to buy a house in Slough and I commuted to New Bond Street every day.

After six months the company had to move from New Bond Street to the centre of Holborn, and suddenly a short bus journey from Paddington station changed to commuting on the underground with its difficulties. There were train delays, bomb hoaxes, fires, and suicide jumpers, and often it was taking me four hours to get to work. Commuting with its increasing costs was causing me stress, and I developed

IBS which when stuck on a crowded train is a problem. A doctor advised me to change my lifestyle as I was also working shifts, and as I had just moved house to Slough I could no longer travel in time and money. So I left the company and took temping work in and around where I was living.

In 1997, I joined a local social group and met Mike my partner, now of 23 years, and I moved in with him at the end of that year and we bought our house together in Buckinghamshire in 1998. My life changed dramatically as I had a soul mate, I completed a B A degree with the Open University in Social Science in 2002, and then I went back to college to take a career counselling course and I became a Career Guidance Counsellor. Two main things happened during this time; firstly, I did not know that Mike was a Senior Manager in the airline industry and our first holiday together was first-class to Mauritius, a total surprise, as I had never really been abroad before. Secondly, I really enjoyed studying and hoped one day to complete a degree of my choice that was not work related.

In 2004 my mother died and suddenly I was the beneficiary of her house which I sold and I no longer had to work. Mike had retired in 1999 when both of us took part in an archaeological training excavation at Fishbourne Roman Palace, where I found a small Roman object, about 2000 years old, under a Roman road I had been digging up. This small object is still on display in Fishbourne Roman Palace Museum, as a weight possibly for spices. I was hooked! We went on several other archaeological training courses over the next few years.

In 2007, we both studied at Oxford University Department of Continuing Education for a Diploma in British Archaeology where we both took a Roman Archaeology Module; but by this time I had become fascinated by Early Prehistory and Human Evolution, modules which I also took. This Diploma formed the basis of my Natural Sciences Degree with the Open University. So now I have a BA (Open) Degree in Social Science and a BSC (Hons) Degree with the Open University.

I think those conversations I had with my father during his illness sparked in me an inquiring mind and love of studying that eventually helped me coped with family stress, traumas and problems that are still ongoing from time to time with my daughters. So now Mike and I are still studying, or doing our own research, and travelling around the world to pursue our interests. Mike has now a MA and specialises in Roman Archaeology and I still pursue my interest in Human Evolution with Natural Sciences, especially geology. I have also been lucky enough to have flown over several live volcanoes.

I have irregular contact with my daughters and grandchildren, but I am always there for them. However, I now give them enough space to live their lives and to make their own mistakes. It is therefore very important to have your own life after the children have left home, particularly after the intensity of coping with a multiple adoption.

Chapter 24

INSIGHTS

What insights has my adoption experiences and my family history given me to understand myself that could help prospective adoptive parents?

This will be difficult to hear but do not underestimate the desire to have children if you cannot have your own, and adoption seems a great opportunity to have children. Knowing the strength of feeling I had at the time I probably would have gone ahead with the adoption. However, with hindsight I probably would have done some things differently, like insisting and getting help earlier. There might have been a possibility of Sian going into a therapeutic community for a time rather than us, particularly me, coping with her behaviour and her sisters.

It is not a failure if you choose not to adopt, and if you do decide it is right for you to be better prepared.

I left home and went straight into a marriage with little experience of other boyfriends, of independence, or of life generally. So get to know as much about yourself, including your interests, desires and aspirations, as much as possible.

For example, I worked hard to save money for years prior to my Dad's illness to go to Africa to work with animals. My dad even supported my wish, much to my mother's disapproval, and he made contacts with people to help me get there, but obviously his illness took over. Even after he started to recover there was an expectation by everyone that I, being a woman and a daughter, had to stay around.

My saved money went into my marriage and I transferred these expectations towards my husband, and my dreams and support died with my dad when he died aged 50. So question your motives and expectations when you adopt.

Be true to yourself as adoption of older children should not be taken lightly considering their past.

Further insights

Advice to prospective adoptive mothers; your legal status is that mother's should take priority over the welfare of children. Even though, in my case Dave was primarily the one who wanted the adoption as he could not have children. I was the one expected by courts and social workers to be the primary caregiver, in any eventuality, which under a multiple adoption is a huge undertaking, and I was not fully aware of this outcome at the time of fostering or adopting the girls'.

Check and communicate feelings in your relationship to adopt, as expectations and ability to cope is different for each person. Dave in not being honest about not wanting to adopt after fostering the girls left me unsupported, and perhaps the adoption should not have gone ahead.

The divorce did affect the girl's behaviour over and above the behavioural traits from their past. I had expected more co-operation from a co-parenting arrangement and perhaps life would have been different if Dave had helped and supported me more. Perhaps I may not have had move away to save my sanity.

Try not to be everything to everyone especially if you're the main carer, take time out for yourself without feeling guilty. Everyone needs time to recharge their batteries. I actually had more time to myself after the divorce, and with a co-parenting arrangement in place. Recently my son-in-law who works within fostering and adoption told me that he tells prospective parents to put themselves first and then the needs of the children. I replied 'why didn't someone tell me this 39 years ago'!

Know your limits which means being open and honest to yourself as well as to others. I think I was but Dave wasn't.

Question your own expectations to adopt and perspective on family life, and don't believe everything that the social workers tell you, as they have a different agenda and targets to meet, as well as being very busy. Our social workers tried their best at the time, but we were all very naïve.

Ask questions of the social workers as we weren't warned that children who are adopted, however young, will cause extra stress in your life because of their past. Extra stress that we weren't expecting or that the social workers thought we would overcome with time.

Gather all the information you can, know where you can help, and from as many different sources, and check if you really can get the support from the social services after the adoption. Our social workers said they would help, but they moved on thinking we all would be OK, but of course we weren't.

Then we could not get any help from any social workers. The Social Services where we adopted the children said we weren't an ongoing case, nor were we residing in their geographic jurisdiction. The local Social Services said our adoption case was not their responsibility. I'm not sure they would have been much help later, in my experience, with the circumstances surrounding Sian's case.

Accept that fostering is different to adoption. Fostering requires links to biological parents, but I think that adoptive parents are different in trying to provide a stable family life with love for the children, that can be undermined by direct links to their past families. I know I would not have been able to adopt under the new circumstances of contact between the biological parents and with the children so young. I can cope with my daughters' biological mother around now they are grown up but I know I would not have coped when they were little.

Whatever you expect once the children have grown up is to accept their past is always with them. Often there are repeated patterns of behaviour from their past, some obvious as at the time of the adoption, and some not apparent until much later in their lives, or even until they are grown up. I think both my daughters choices of working within the helping professions, maybe a continuation of the past, with strong links to their childhood experiences.

Be aware of your own childhood experiences. I was an only child and therefore did not understand what was normal sibling rivalry, compared to the level of bullying, guilt, and jealousy, between my girls that was more related to their past. This became apparent recently when Tiffany won some money, in feelings Becca had towards her biological mother, and the negative consequences after Tiffany's Wedding Party.

There is an additional complication with a multiple adoption that social workers do not make clear to prospective parents: it is called a 'Life Story Book', which is built up over time with an adopted child. What that means is you build up a book as you answer an individual child's questions about their past, honestly and as truthfully as you can, according to their age, to help them put their life in perspective. It should be done under social work supervision. However, it doesn't take into consideration that the children in a multiple adoption will talk to each other and create stories that are not true. These siblings believe each other more strongly than they believe you or past social workers.

Access to professionals, is important, who understand psychology and the behaviour of adopted children, and they can provide strategies to help adoptive parents deal with difficult childhood behaviour. Perhaps in our case a multiple adoption was not right for these children as Sian really need therapeutic care and Tiffany really needed to be away from the influence of her sisters and their behaviour.

Social workers need to tell adoptive parents it is OK to take some care of themselves as they are looking after damaged children. They also should tell adoptive parents that they cannot repair the damage done to the children prior to having them.

However, family life can be fun and children can thrive. Becca and Tiffany have done well in their professions and Becca has a degree. However, adoptive children are not you own biological flesh and blood and they come with a past, where you cannot make as much difference as you think. Always in the background is the child's heritage and their biological family's medical history, as my daughters and I are discovering today.

Do not underestimate that with a return of a biological mother that a birth mother may take priority over you, as Becca said to me 'She gave birth to us', despite all the love and care you tried to give them over the years. At the moment I have closer relationships with my grandchildren than I do with my daughters.

Be aware of the life you may have to give up. I have been lucky in that I was young at the time of the adoption, and the children were young. So that when they grew up I had a chance to study and travel that perhaps I should have had in the beginning.

Do make sure you maintain outside interests if you can so you can look after yourself when the children are older and left home. I have met many mothers who feel there is no life after the children have left home. There is education, hobbies, interests and voluntary work to give your life meaning, especially after such an intense time bringing up children within a multiple adoption.

Both Mike and I have reawakened our childhood interests into study and travel.

Looking back I feel I was motivated in my decisions by guilt, but I did my best and I no longer feel guilty about past events. That is all anyone can do as an adoptive mum.

Update

On the 23rd November 2020, at Parliament Questions: A House of Commons question on adoption was put by Edward Timpson to Gavin Williamson, the Education Secretary. Edward Timpson stated that 600 potential adoptions had been held up by Government processes, and raised the question. "When will these children find their 'Forever Families?'"

Gavin Williamson replied "the Government are setting up a Recruitment Programme to help these children find their 'Forever Homes'".

I must admit I do not like the terminology of 'Forever Families' or 'Forever Homes', as I think this perpetuates a myth that adoption is wonderful for all concerned. Though many do succeed, when you consider that out of 600 potential adoptions up to 25% can break down, with so much distress and misery, greater help and realism is needed by all.

The BBC (2019) wrote an article about an adoptive mum who had to be treated for Post-Traumatic Stress Disorder (PTSD) because of the violent behaviour from her adopted daughter. There are many such stories of Adoption Breakdown and mine nearly broke down several times too.

To the Government: Please think about the cost of helping adoptive families in trouble when compared to the cost of keeping children in care.

To all Adoptive Mums: You are not alone. Fight for the help when you need it. Adoption Breakdowns are not your fault!

CONCLUSION

I have found writing this memoir a cathartic release from huge psychological stress and it has improved my physical health. I found writing it with the research very therapeutic as it was a case of 'Counsellor heal thyself'. This is true as I am now 70 years old and can face the future without guilt and my daughters can face theirs with my love.

Between Mike and I we now have five daughters, nine grandchildren and I have one great grandchild.

I am often asked was adopting the girls worth it. Yes, in my case, as for all the problems and traumas I still love them dearly; I have great relationships with all my grandchildren and I am proud to be a great-grandmother. Whenever I have been in doubt about my daughters or the adoption I remember those three little girls standing in my lounge, with their boxes of worldly goods and dirty dogged eared toys, full of expectations, and my heart goes out to them again.

FURTHER SOURCES OF HELP

Adoption UK: A Service for adoptive families. Units 11 & 12, Vantage Business Park, Bloxham Road, Banbury, OX16 9UX. 01295 752240. info@adoptionuk.org.uk

Barnardo's Adoption Agency: are now one of the largest adoption agencies and they do offer follow up support. www.barnardos.org.uk

British Agencies for Adoption and Fostering (2000) three Advice Notes booklets entitled; Child From the Past, If you are Adopted, and Talking about Origins

Child Adoption: GOV.UK. Provides information on all aspects of adoption from legal details and early stage assessments etc.

Citizens Advice: Offers advice on the telephone or can search for a local citizen's advice bureau. https://www.citizensadvice.org.uk National Advice Line: 03444 111 4444.

CoramBAAF Adoption and Fostering Academy. The Adoption and Fostering Agency that I got my information from is now closed and had been transferred to CORAM (BAAF) which is the British Association of Adoption and Fostering. https://corambaaf.org.uk

Department of Education – GOV.UK. The Department produces a series of topics on Fostering and Adoption entitled: Research in Practice.

https://fosteringandadoption.rip.org.uk/topics/attachment-theory-research/

Department of Health and Social Care – GOV.UK: www.gov.uk

Family Mediation Services: They help with family conflict issues, and I think they now cover family conciliation. They may advise the court on co-parenting arrangements as our family conciliation advisers or they may give you advice for next steps. You need to find one in your local area.

Find my Past: www.findmypast.co.uk

IOW Family History Society: www.isle-of-wight-fhs-co.uk

NORCAP was an organisation that help trace birth parents based in Oxfordshire. (The **NORCAP** Contact Register has been transferred over to **Family Action,** as of 4th of April 2020).

NSPCC for Adults concerned about a child. Weston House, 42 Curtain Road, London, EC2A 3NH. 0808 800 5000.

Relate: Marriage and relationship guidance. Can help find local counsellors. www.relate.org.uk

For Adoption in your local area or in different counties use **GOV. UK**. For example www.hants.gov.uk

REFERENCES

Arsivi N. P. (2015) Childhood Traumatic Experiences, Anxiety, and Depression Levels in Fibromyalgia and Rheumatoid Arthritis. Pp 344-349.

BBC News (2019) Adoption Breakdown: 'No support' for violent children. 28th October 2019.
https://www.bbc.co.uk/news/uk-england-50083910

Care for the Family (2020) Attachment Issues and Developmental Trauma.
https://careforthefamily.org.uk/family-life/parent-support

Department of Health. The Adoption Contact Register-Information for Adopted People and their Relatives. Access to Birth Records-Information for Adopted people in the UK. I have old copies of these booklets but there should be ones related to the updated Children's Act. They list on the back current organisations that will help and support you.

I could not at the time find any booklets at that time that would help adoptive parents.

Family Action (2020) now holds the **NORCAP Contact Register.** https://www.family-action.org.uk

First for Adoption (2019) Contact in adoption: making sense of the past. Helps you find adoption agencies in your area. https://www.first4adoption.org.uk/being-an-adoptive-parent/

Focus on the family (2020) Attachment: What adoptive families need to know.

https://www.focusonthefamily.ca/content/attachment-what-adoptive-families-need-to-know

Harte, A & Drinkwater, D. (2017). Over a quarter of adoptive families in crisis, survey shows.
https://www.bbc.co.uk/news/uk-4137942#targetText=Modernadoption,childrenareadoptedeveryyear/

Holden N.L (1991) Adoption and Eating Disorders: A High Risk Group. The British Journal of Psychiatry: London. Vol 158, ISS.6 June 1991

Kay, C., Green, J., Sharma, K. (2016) Disinhibited Attachment Disorder in UK Adopted Children During Middle Childhood: Prevalence Validity and Possible Development Origin. Journal of Abnormal Child Psychology. Vol. 44 pp. 1375-1386 (2016).

Muir, H., Moorhead, J. (2010) The Truth about Inter-Racial Adoption. The Guardian. Wed.3rd Nov 2010.

Support not Separation (2020 Disrupted Adoptions-What Councils Don't Want You To Know.
http://supportnotseparation.blog/2020/02/13/disrupted-adoptions-what-councils-don't-want-you-to-know/

The advantage with this site is it reviews the updated problems around adoption and gives a full range of further references.

Warwick University (2020). Borstal.
warwick.ac.uk/services/library/mrc/archives_online/digital/
prison/borstal/. Accessed 17th December 2020.

**Westermeyer, J., Yoon, G., Amundson, C., Warwick,
M., Kuskowski, M.A. (2015)** Personality disorders in
adopted versus non-adopted adults. Psychiatry Res. 2015
Apr.30. Accessed through Elsevier (14/092020).